Qualitative Inquiry in Social Work
Global Perspectives
Vol 1(1) 13 August 2018

Inquiry for a Just and Caring World

Welcome to the first issue of *Qualitative Inquiry in Social Work*. This is a global publication that bridges gaps between oral transmission and journal articles. The writing will be informal, personal, and interesting and will match our experiences as qualitative inquirers.

We chose the word "inquiry" over "research" because the term "inquiry" has a broad sweep that includes research and goes beyond it. Jim Drisko wrote about the nature of inquiry in his article for this issue. He said inquiry involves fun, creativity, wonder, and speculation.

The articles in *QISW* will have these qualities. Such writing makes ideas accessible to a wide audience. Think about what's in your fieldnotes, the kinds of things you say about your research in relaxed settings, and what you think about but don't write down or even talk about. That's what we want for *QISW*.

QISW is a publication of the Qualitative Social Work Global Network that arose from Social Work Day, the great qualitative social work get-together that happens each May at the International Congress of Qualitative Inquiry, in Urbana, Illinois, USA. Norman Denzin is the originator of ICQI.

Qualitative inquiry includes reflections, speculations, theorizing, and creating accounts not only of human phenomena but also how our efforts might bring about positive social change. See the articles in this first issue for an idea of what I mean. Join us.

Jane Gilgun, editor
gilgun@ umn.edu

Karen Staller was Keynote Speaker at ICQI

Karen Staller wuth Norman Denzin at the opening plenary of the International Congress of Qualitative Inqury

Karen Staller, Unversity of Michigan, Ann Arbor, USA, was a keynote speaker at the opening plenary of the 14th Annual International Congress of Qualitative Inquiry (ICQI), held each year in Urbana, Illinois, USA. Her address was called Stitching Tattered Cloth: Reflections on Social Justice and Qualitative Inquiry in Troubled Times. Karen based her address on archival research she is conducting at the Children's Aide Society in New York City, USA. She showed how qualitative inquiry has moral, ethical, and political dimensions.

Karen shared the work of Charles Loring Brace (1826-1890), a nineteenth century social worker who lived during troubled times in the United States, and made comparisons for how we as social workers and other applied qualitative inquirers respond to our own troubled times.

Debra Nelson Gardell said of Karen's keynote, "My pride in anticipating and then watching a social worker, Dr. Karen Staller, in front of a group of intellectuals I admire, respect, and value swelled my heart." Read Debra's full article by clicking here.

Here is a link to an audiofile of Karen's keynote speech. https://goo.gl/p1FhoZ. Karen is also co-editor of *Qualitative Social Work: Research & Practice* and a co-founder of Social Work Day.

Qualitative Inquiry in Social Work
Global Perspectives

Qualitative Inquiry in Social Work is a place where scholars throughout the world share what they experience, learn, and do in their local contexts. We welcome stories, reflections, speculations, insights, hopes, dreams, poetry, performances, photographs, ideas for new endeavors, solicitations of ideas for projects, and any other topic relevant to social work. Social work benefits from the exchange of ideas.

For the next issue, we will feature What's Going on in Your Home Regions, that will be a set of articles on issues authors see in their local contexts and how qualitative inquiry has played or could play a part. See also the invitation to submit articles and guidelines for writing. Of special note is a call for papers for a special collection to appear in *Qualitative Social Work: Research and Practice*.

Qualitative Inquiry in Social Work (QISW) is an occasional publication of the Qualitative Social Work Global Network, an association of social workers whose home base is the International Association of Qualitative Inquiry located in Urbana, IL, USA, Norman Denzin, founder. If you would like to join the Global Network and be on the mailing list, send an email to QUAL-SW-GLOBAL-NETWORK@listserv.ua.edu.

Purpose

The purpose of *QISW* is to provide a place for social work qualitative inquirers throughout the world to exchange ideas. Ideas arise from experiences within local contexts. *Qualitative Inquiry in Social Work* welcomes stories, reflections, speculations, thought pieces, hopes, dreams, ideas for new endeavors, solicitations of ideas for various projects, and any other topic relevant to social work and qualitative inquiry.

The global reach of *QISW* will allow social workers in a variety of settings to learn from each other. For instance, the issues that Chilean social work researchers encounter can enlighten the thinking and procedures of researchers in many other local settings.

The articles sometimes will be published in the first language of the authors so that persons who do not speak English will have access to these articles. Spelling depends upon authors' version of the English they use.

Who Knows?

This issue is the first of what could be a few more or many more. We don't know what if any influence this publication will have. We go forward, confident in knowing that nothing is as practical as good ideas. Good ideas are leaven that promote a just and caring world. The sources of our ideas are global. No matter the future of *QISW*, the ideas will contribute to just and caring societies.

Types of Articles

Articles are from 50 to 500 words and sometimes longer on any topic relevant to qualitative inquiry in social work. We welcome articles from service providers, service users, researchers, policy makers, program planners, community organizers, academics, and anyone else interested in contributing to qualitative inquiry in social work. Click here for guidelines for writing for *QISW*.

Table of Contents

Stitching Tattered Cloth in Action: *QISW* and #ICQIcarryitforward

Karen Staller
University of Michigan, Ann Arbor, USA
kstaller@umich.edu

Leave it to Jane Gilgun, the fearless leader of the social work contingent at ICQI, to come up with the idea for a newsletter, *Qualitative Inquiry in Social Work (QISW)*, as well as to launch it within 48  hours of the 2018 Congress. Jane has been the epitome of social-work-in-action since the beginning. Her focused energy has always been the lifeblood of the considerable social work presence at ICQI.

I would like to use my little 200-word space to fully embrace this new endeavor. This year, I was honored to deliver the keynote address at the Congress in an address I called Stitching Tattered Cloth: Reflections on Social Justice and Qualitative Inquiry in Troubled Times.

My central message was that by uniting our scattered voices we can actualize Norman Denzin's vision for ICQI as a global political movement using qualitative inquiry as a transformative force in social justice work.

Agents of Positive Social Change

We can be agents of positive social change as well as actors in resistance movements. This newsletter offers a means to realize that vision by providing a space to both share, and unite, our voices. Of course, it took Jane, the consummate social worker, to put a hypothetical idea into motion.

Here is a link to an audiophile of Karen's keynote speech. https://goo.gl/p1FhoZ Back to ToC

Reflections on Karen Staller's Keynote Speech #ICQICarryItForward

Taylor Ellis
University of Alabama, Tuscaloosa, USA
tjellis1@crimson.ua.edu

This was the second time that I have attended ICQI and it was particularly special because after experiencing wonderful presentations throughout Social Work Day, I was able to hear our very own Dr. Karen Staller give one of the two keynote speeches.

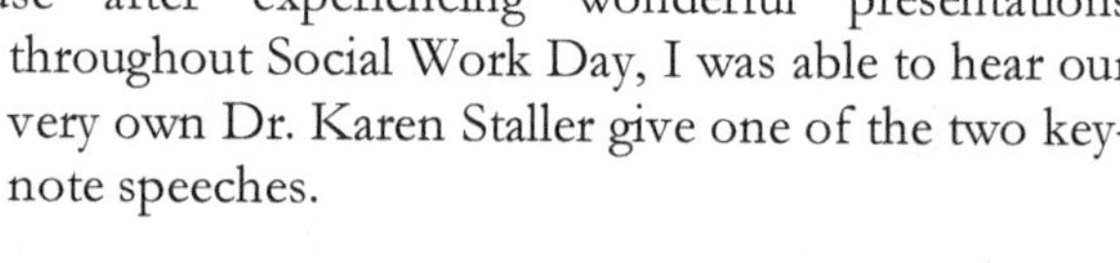

Standing Room Only

I listened as Dr. Staller spoke into a space that was standing room only and filled the hallway outside of the room. However, I did not only listen; I felt. I felt relief as Dr. Staller made connections to our current political and social climate and those of bygone eras that we as a nation survived.

Stories

I felt excited as she told the story of Charles Loring Brace who chose to question societal standards and assessed how to use his position in society as leverage for the betterment of others. I felt hope as Dr. Staller reminded each of us in and outside of the room that we as qualitative researchers operate in a space of listening to the voice of others, challenging the status quo, and although we may often feel alone in our endeavors we need only to look around at the people in the room and be reminded that we are in this fight together.

Dr. Staller left us with the charge of #ICQICarryItForward, a hastag for Twitter. A hashtag is similar to what we call a category in qualitative research in that it allows people to group posts, tweets, stories, etc. on various social media platforms.

Hashtags

Typically, hashtags become links for other users to click on and see other posts labeled with that same hashtag. Dr. Staller presented several hashtags, including #ICQIGlobalAction, #ICQIEvidence, #ICQIUnite and others.

However, #ICQICarryItForward stuck with me, because as the speech ended, I could not help but smile, feeling invigorated, comforted, and compelled to write, to carry it forward. Therefore, I generated this simple but poignant haiku inspired by Dr. Staller's speech:

What is the world if
it cannot be critiqued?
Stagnant; lifeless.

Note: Taylor participated in a three-minute thesis competition at the University of Alabama, Tuscaloosa, USA, in 2017. His title was Healing Through Poetry: Writing Towards a Sacred Community. Here's a link. https://youtu.be/OqGx1H5799o

Social Work Day

Social Work Day takes place each year as a pre-conference at the International Congress of Qualitative Inquiry (ICQI), held at the University of Illinois, Urbana, Il, USA. This section of *QISW* is a collection of reflections on Social Work Day 2018 that began with a plenary panel composed of PhD students. The topic was Social Work for the Common Good.

With an opening and closing plenary and four concurrent sessions with four to five panels each, we covered many subjects, such as research with indigenous and refugee populations, intersectionality and women's experience, privilege and resistance, arts-based inquiry, critical inquiry, participatory action research, and social work-specific research. Click here for a link to the program.

A Site for Research

Two PhD students, Catherine Kramer and Darren Cosgrove conducted research at Social Work Day. They wrote about their research here. I hope that participants continue so see Social Work Day (SWD0 and ICQI as sites for research.

At this year's SWD, Jim Drisko speculated about the differences between inquiry and research. Inquiry includes and goes beyond research and involves, creativity, speculations, and innovative ways of doing and disseminating research. As Jim talked about inquiry, I realized the time had come for a newsletter on qualitative inquiry in social work from Social Work Day. This year's program is available on Amazon. Jim's thinking about inquiry in social work is in this issue of *QISW*.

What's in This Issue

This issue begins with an introduction to *QISW* and with the great news that Karen Staller, a social work educator and inquirer, was a keynote speaker at ICQI this year. The articles include reflections on Social Work Day 2018, writings on aspects of qualitative inquiry, a call for papers for a special collection of papers presented at Social Work Day, an announcement of the Ask Dr. Debra column, news and notes, a history of Social Work Day, an introduction of the editors of *QISW*, and invitations and guidelines to contribute to *QISW*.

Reflections
on Social Work Day 2018

Research as Personal and Political

Anindita Bhattacharya
Columbia University, New York, USA
ab4050@columbia.edu

This year's Social Work Day at the International Congress of Qualitative Inquiry (ICQI) brought social workers together from various parts of the  globe to discuss how our research serves the common good. The conference encouraged us to critically reflect on the process of doing qualitative research, paying close attention to how our personal selves shape research and in turn are impacted by it.

As a social worker and researcher, I question how can we assess the impact our research makes? I believe that as social work researchers, we have the moral responsibility to do research that moves beyond knowledge creation and integrates a transformative and emancipatory agenda for marginalized communities.

The Gendered Personal

I was the third girl born to my parents in a patriarchal culture that to date has a son preference and devalues women. My mother's story and the gender-based discrimination (limited educational opportunities and early marriage) she experienced significantly shaped my worldview.

My mother's experiences with depression also made me aware of power laden mental health practices in India. Mental health practitioners focused solely on my mother's diagnosis and subdued her experiences and the social context that had withheld her fundamental right to make independent choices for her own well-being.

The Gendered Social

I witnessed similar gendered narratives when I worked as a social worker for women with serious mental illness (SMI) admitted to psychiatric institutions in India. Several gender related contextual factors (e.g. interpersonal violence, limited autonomy and family abandonment) served to keep women isolated in psychiatric institutions indefinitely, deterring their reintegration with communities. The discrimination that women experienced in families and communities was further exacerbated by psychiatric institutions that silenced their voices and reduced them to passive beings within treatment spaces.

Personal and Political

As a feminist researcher, I perceive research to be both personal and political. I cannot see women's experiences in a vacuum. Instead, I see them as an outcome of power inequities and therefore take careful measures to ensure that my research does not recreate and reinforce oppressive structures that women already exist within. I advocate for alternative ways to understanding women's illness experiences; methodologies that prioritise women's realities.

In my dissertation, I explore narratives of women, devoid of family support who have lived in institutions in dire circumstances and are currently residing at a half way home, to examine how the intersection of gender and other marginalized identities shape their life experiences.

Using women's voices as the starting point, I envision developing gender sensitive mental health research and practice that are grounded in women's contexts and experiences.

Social Work Day

I value an academic space like Social Work Day and ICQI that provides an intellectually invigorating and nurturing environment to foster growth among early career scholars. It is incredible to meet and network with scholars whose research we look up to, who through their writings and action have redefined knowledge, rigor and validity in research, who encourage the use of personal selves in the research process, and most importantly reinforce the impact and significance of qualitative research in social work. I look forward to Social Work Day and ICQI 2019!

De-Colonizing My Mind at Social Work Day

Stephen T. Wilson
University of Washington, Seattle, USA
wilsonst@uw.edu

The first time I attended Social Work Day at ICQI was in 2011 at the suggestion of my instructor, Dr. James Drisko, who told me a paper I had  written on jazz and intersubjectivity while in my doctoral residence at Smith College was something to present at a conference. I was surprised he had suggested this option in that the paper was an assignment, centering on how I viewed my work as a clinician. I had not anticipated my instructor, Dr. Lourdes Mattei, would be enamored and recommend the paper to Dr. Drisko.

Jazzed

Presenting a paper about my ideas was a new experience for me. I was, so to speak, jazzed and a bit anxious. I was also astonished and pleased that I had extra time when two presenters cancelled.

In 2018, I once again presented at Social Work Day, this time from my dissertation whose title is An Exploration of Race and Ethnicity for Multiracial Individuals Adopted Transracially. I was simultaneously anxious and excited at the possibility of sharing my work with colleagues. It had been rare that I had called myself a scholar. Yet, there I was at an international conference sharing my work with other scholars as a scholar.

Belonging

I have to admit, it took a bit of mind twisting to claim my space there, to distance myself from feeling like I really didn't belong. The very act of being there was a personal act of de-colonizing my mind.

My presentation went okay. I usually bring my own AV connectors and chose not to. When I got to the presentation room, there were connectors available, but I didn't trust them enough and instead chose to trust my abilities as a presenter. I gave the presentation without my equipment and "improvised," if you will.

The truth is I missed a few points, and right as I sat down, I began critiquing myself. "You missed this. You didn't say that? Wow. Ten minutes is really a short time. Why did you choose to forefront your intersectional identities? Did that take away time from your data and the meat of your work?"?

My Agency

Given feedback later from one of my mentors, the answer to the last question was yes. I had indeed taken time away from the meat of my work to explain why I had agency in the research at all.

Sometimes, the researcher identity statement can detract from the work itself. The real issue here for me was to privilege key informants' voices, to tell their stories, to bring them to life in those few precious moments, those ten minutes.

The Potency of Black Colonialization

In reflecting, I have to ask myself what part of my not feeling I belonged there got in my way of being more effective? How does my downplaying or stating my place in this conference personally disempower me? Boy, Black colonization is potent. When you believe the story that questions your place in the academy, no one else has to question you, Steve, you're doing it yourself; I was playing party to the lie that I didn't really belong there.

Yet, there I was…

When we got together at the end of Social Work Day at the Town Hall to discuss how the day had gone I noticed I was different. I was speaking, lending my voice to the discussions. I often wonder whether I talk too much. Am I standing on my cis-gendered male privilege and inserting myself where I'm not always needed?

Saying What I Wanted to Say

I finally decided to just let that go and say what I had to say. I was particularly touched by the discussions on intersectionality, multiple identities, and how assumed identity was simultaneously potent as a means of social advocacy and a place of power.

Then it happened: A question that I was sure I could not just sit back and be an observer. I could not be quiet. The question was about identity and its impact on key informants. Dr. Jane Gilgun inquired about what she might be missing as researcher, with a history of interviewing Black men. What was she missing?

Images of Black Men

I heard myself speak up from an internal space that I know well: how other people view me as a Black man. Angry, hyper-sexual, uneducated, incarcerated, and host of other derogatory statements. I was acutely aware that those images were a part of some people's beliefs about who I am, and how potent that colonizing action is. I think Dr. WEB DuBois calls it double consciousness.

It is a peculiar sensation, this double-consciousness, this sense of always looking at one's self through the eyes of others... One ever feels [h]is twoness, An American, a Negro; two should, two thoughts, two unrecognized. Strivings; two warring ideals in one dark body, whose dogged strength. Alone keeps it from being torn asunder.

Personal Agency

As I listened to myself talking, I wasn't struggling. I was stating an experience: my experience. Not someone else's experience, mine. I was privileging me. Putting my voice into the room. I was the Key Informant. This for me is where the potency of making my voice known. Putting it into the room without reservation was an act of personal agency, a way to claim power and speak for those who cannot always speak for themselves. A part of my teaching is reminding students that we as social workers can speak when others are disempowered, not for them, but with and on their behalf.

That said, I really appreciated the pop-up session on race and research that I participated in with Tom Kenemore and Jane Gilgun. Across differences of race, age, and gender, we spoke from our hearts and shared vulnerabilities. I felt like I belonged and realized I was indeed supposed to be there.

Citation

DuBois, W. E. B. (1903), On our spiritual strivings[STW1]. In David Lewis (Ed). *W.E.B. DuBois: A Reader[STW2]* (p. 29). New York: Holt.

Engaging Self, Otherness, and Reflexivity:
A Caribbean Social Worker's Reflections

Tracie Rogers
University of the Southern Caribbean
Trinidad and Tobago, West Indies
tracie.rogers@gmail.com

… [I]dentities are the names we give to the different ways we are positioned by, and position ourselves within, the narratives of the past… only from this [second] position [that] we can properly understand the traumatic character of "the colonial experience." The ways in which black people, black experiences, were positioned and subject-ed in the dominant regimes of representation were the effects of a critical exercise of cultural power and normalization…They had the power to make us see and experience ourselves as "Other." Hall (1990, p. 223)

The moment I enter United States immigration, I am aware of myself as "Other." It is a tangible, visceral sentiment. I am aware of my positionality,

as well as my imaginations of the various ways in which I am positioned in the eyes of others. When I entered the US for my second International Congress of Qualitative Inquiry (ICQI) conference in May 2018, the barking of an immigration official was the first materialization of my expectations for these trips. She bellowed at me to enter a line that I know I should not enter.

Oppositional Thoughts

I have made my way through US immigration countless times over the past 20 years; either for conferences, visiting family members, or as an international student. I was certain that I have had more experience with US immigration than this officer. I entertained the thought of informing her of where I should go but quickly dismissed it, because I know better than to offer an oppositional thought at immigration1.

This officer had minimal authority with maximum potential to delay my journey; I have learned that it is best to save my energy for engagement with the officer responsible for processing my entry. Surely, my identities as social work researcher, teacher and academic should mitigate feelings of powerlessness in the situation.

The truth is, as I was being bullied into the wrong immigration line, I was mindful of the performance that would likely ensue if I asserted myself. I weighed whether it would cost me more time than being in the wrong line with thoughts of the short time between my connections. I recall clasping my 7-year old daughter's hand tightly and wondering how she imagined me for the brief moments of this encounter. I then proceeded to waste 25 minutes in the wrong line.

Power, Privilege, & Representation

By the start of ICQI's 2018 Social Work Day, I had a dozen comparable experiences of this running internal dialogue about the performance and imaginations of power, privilege and representations. Unpacking and repacking internal narratives of 'difference' and 'other' is the intellectual work of international conferences for me. As I crept into the opening plenary, Social Work and the Common Good, I was still reeling from an incident that occurred the previous day at the conference registration desk.

An African student working at the registration desk was beaming at me when he realised I was from the Caribbean and then specifically, Trinidad and Tobago. There was warmth and familiarity, as if we were reuniting, although we had never met. This type of experience when crossing paths with people in the Diaspora is not the rule, but it happens more often than not.

We were quickly interrupted by a white American female conference administrator, who interjected with, "I can't see what you two have in common. You are from completely different parts of the world." She outstretched both of her arms in a diagonal direction, cupping each of her hands to signify how far apart our geographical origins were; she shook her head with astonishment that the two of us could actually believe we had any commonalities.

Vexing My Spirit

Her manner was dismissive and tone authoritative and it broke the stride of our conversation. I felt the student recoil as he started to stutter, all the time maintaining a placid smile. His response was familiar and I imagined the power dynamics that played in his head perhaps included considerations of his status as African, minority, foreigner and student.

The woman continued her ramble about the distance between West Africa and the West Indies with a confidence and authority that maddened me or rather, to use a Trinidadian colloquialism, "vexed my spirit." "But you have no idea about our connections in the Diaspora. It is a powerful force and we know it."

Colonial Wheeling

My tone was firm and I maintained eye contact with the student as I spoke. She continued babbling. I stopped listening. I interpreted her persistence as yet another exercise of colonial wheeling of an assumed power to craft the experience of ourselves as "Other." I took a deep breath, ignored her invasion and gave my best wishes to the student.

I reached for my daughter's hand. Again. Again? She was an arm's length away, leaned over the registration table, making her own name tag. There was an African-American student who earlier marveled over my daughter's dreadlocks, holding the name tag flat as she wrote her name. Yet another experience to unpack, as my daughter who wears a resistance identity on her head, was marking herself present at the conference.

Cultural Power, Representation, & Resistance

Stuart Hall's seminal work exploring cultural identity for the Caribbean subject felt particularly pertinent in this seemingly benign incident, as a member of a majority culture assumed the 'right' to dictate the identity and connection of two persons of colour.

I was still digesting the representations of identity at that registration table. The various ways in which cultural power, normalization, and resistance interacted in that incident consumed my thoughts as I listened to Jane Gilgun's opening remarks. I started identifying the common thread running from my experience at the US port of entry, to this entry into an academic space committed this year to, Qualitative Inquiry in Troubled Times.

Discourses of Social Work Day

The discourses of 2018 Social Work Day were particularly significant and enlightening to me because it pushed me out of my comfort zone. As disturbing as my experiences of cultural othering had been from my arrival to the US, it was also familiar and cosy. When I attend international conferences in the US, as well as other parts of the world, I am prepared for my inner filter to be in overdrive.

A Caribbean Sensibility

I hear discourses with a Caribbean sensibility--specifically as a citizen of Trinidad and Tobago with its history of predominantly English colonial rule, genocide of Tainos/native peoples, importation and enslavement of African peoples, indentured East Indian labourers, waves of migration from Syria and China, creolization, pluralism, an oil and natural gas producing state with little historical focus on tourism.

I received information through this filter, with the awareness that I hear and process discussions as an 'Other.' While I can identify with the experiences of other traditionally oppressed black bodies, I am aware that my black Caribbean body is different and has less visibility.

I translate the discourses, and pull out the significance for minority positionality, but I share very little of it in discussions at panels. I have the distinct sense that I am not seen in these spaces and in retrospect I now realise that I have subconsciously decided not to show up either--at least not with the full array of my identity.

As I reflect on this experience of ICQI, I can identify how I show up as social worker and researcher, perceiving little space for my other identities in international conferences. Who there will understand? Why would my "I" matter in this academic space? In response, I silence myself and prepare to engage my thoughts with like-minded persons, like my Haitian-American colleague Cynthia Langtiw, who I met a few years ago at another conference.

Discourse Spaces

At this conference, I randomly found my way into discourse spaces with other academics of colour on other special interest groups (SIGs) (I had phenomenal conversations with Kakali Bhattacharya and Venus Evans-Winters sitting under a tree in the quadrangle). I am not saying that similar conversations are not had amongst academics at the social work SIG; I am only saying that I have not been party to them.

Another level of "Other" I perceive in social work spaces comes from my professional identity as a drama therapist. I am an artist, a former dancer (my knees are just not what they used to be) and a poet. In the past, I have struggled to reconcile my identities as social worker and creative arts therapist. I have often found myself in a peculiar "in between" space, where my creative arts therapy and social work disciplines did not cross paths. At this intersection, I learned and continue to learn, the value of diversity of methods, reflexivity, culturally situated practice and integrity to personal process.

Perhaps this is one reason I am so easily seduced by the arts-based research SIGs. I seem not to be able to find "my people" in social work academic spaces. Three years prior, my ICQI Social Work Day was marked by polite, passionate and articulate academics, who were driven to help and make the world a better place with action. There was little focus on critical theory or diversity of methods. I did not experience the space as subversive or diverse.

2018 Social Work Day was strikingly different.

Beginning with the opening plenary, which only featured students (one of whom is a drama therapist--the wonderful Christine Mayor) to the bold impassioned assertion by Stephen Wilson at the closing plenary--"If you do not see my colour, then you do not see me", Social Work Day 2018 was as a millennial would describe it, "Lit" (sic). Throughout the day, positionalities were placed on the table as part of core research processes rather than a checked box.

Discussions included intriguing perspectives on reflexivity, decolonization, and post-colonialism. There was less filtering, and I felt myself melt into a space where I began to feel comfort. The time felt too short, and I was in a twist about what to attend. My colleague Cynthia took charge of my daughter for most of that day. When my daughter was with me, I felt pride that she could see me present in this space, engaging in these discussions; when she was not there, I wished I could reach for her hand.

Much Progress to be Made
It is not my intention to romanticise Social Work Day 2018. There is so much progress to be made and as more people take liberties in discussing "whiteness" I am curious about how other black bodies hear that discourse. As a black body, I have been processing "blackness" and "otherness" somewhat silently in this space and similar spaces, and now that race is being tabled, I wonder, how do we address the vastness of this concept in a nuanced, situated and just manner.

More CRT at Social Work Day
Jane Gilgun ended the closing plenary with a call for greater engagement in critical theory and critical race theory as we engage in social work research and scholarship. I am excited about the prospect of how this practice-based and academic discipline working towards the liberation of people (IFSW, 2014), can stretch its imaginations at the next Congress.

As I reflect on Social Work Day, I take responsibility for my silence and complicity. Now is the time to actively seek out alliances, articulate minority perspectives and engage in more academic discourse and writing. I look forward to a Social Work Day ICQI 2019 driven by this momentum, as I continue to reach for my daughter's hand.

Citations

Hall, Stuart (1990) 'Cultural identity and diaspora' in Jonathan Rutherford (ed.) *Identity: community, culture, difference.* London: Lawrence & Wishart

International Federation of Social Workers (2014). Proposed Global Definition of Social Work. Retrieved from http://ifsw.org/get-involved/global-definition-of-social-work/

Engagement in Reflexivity & Contextual Awareness

David Camacho
Columbia University, New York, USA
dc3027@columbia.edu

ICQI Social Work Day provided an opportunity to bring to the forefront the science of qualitative inquiry. This year's diverse scholarly presentations were an affirmation of the critical need for us as responsible knowledge creators to engage in processes of personal reflexivity and contextual awareness.

Knowledge creation is not random and never fully objective. Often our research is personal; we address sensitive topics and carry the torch for marginalized communities in politically oppressive contexts. Thus, we as social work researchers must constantly reflect on how our unique experiences shape the who, where, what, when, why and how we research and most importantly the knowledge we produce.

Personal Experiences

My personal experiences shape my lenses as a social work researcher. I use research as an advocacy tool to address contemporary issues of power, race, oppression and privilege and their effects on the physical and mental health needs of ethnic and sexual minority older adults. My work is greatly influenced by my 15-year journey as a caregiver to my Mexican parents. Numerous interactions with healthcare providers through often under-resourced and fragmented health care systems in

East Los Angeles motivate my desire to develop and implement interventions to improve the physical and emotional well-being of minority older adults.

In addition, my own experiences as a Mexican-American gay man and my frequent navigation of predominantly white and heterosexual spaces enhance my awareness that race, sexual orientation and their intersection shape lived experiences and influence health.

Power, Race, Oppression, & Privilege

Furthermore, in today's political climate, immigrants, people of color and LGBT communities are often targets of institutional and physical violence.

These incidents are a critical reminder that as social work researchers, we cannot afford to simply create knowledge. Instead we must be keenly aware of how power, race, oppression and privilege shapes our work and the impact it will have across 'real world' settings.

A Network of Scholars

Finally, ICQI is an invaluable bridge to a support network of scholars. As a current doctoral student, I relished the opportunities to engage with senior scholars who not only understand the power of qualitative scholarship but are also willing to guide the next generation of scholars. I look forward to participating in future ICQI meetings and contributing to its growth in years to come.

Social Work Day as a Site for Data Collection

Darren Cosgrove & Catherine Kramer
Welfare, University at Albany—SUNY
dcosgrove@albany.edu
ckramer@albany.edu

As emerging social work researchers, we are interested in the use of community-centered and transformative research methodologies. We  share a commitment to the use of participatory action research (PAR) or community-based participatory research (CBPR) methods and benefitted from faculty mentors who have supported our exploration of the alignment between social work values (e.g. service, self-determination and social justice) and the principles of these methodologies (e.g. shared knowledge generation and social action). We are inspired by how PAR and CBPR link research to practice, which is consistent with an applied field of study like social work. Despite the parallels, these methods are underrepresented within social work's research literature.

Why Not More PAR/CBPR?

Curious about the reasons for such underrepresentation, we hoped to organize a panel discussion at Social Work Day on action research methodologies among early career social work scholars. Ultimately, we shifted from a panel to a data collection workshop as part of a larger research study to better capture a range of experiences and widely disseminate the findings. The workshop provided the opportunity to engage in collaborative inquiry with early career social work scholars on their motivations for pursuing participatory research methods, as well as the factors that serve as facilitators and barriers to their work. In addition, we conducted interviews leading up to, during and after Social Work Day, which was a pre-conference and the main conference, the International Congress of Qualitative Inquiry, to explore these experiences in-depth.

IRB Issues

To ensure ease in our IRB approval process, we contacted an IRB staff member who helped us identify and think through how we would address ethnical challenges with collecting research in a conference setting. The main concern was that those who attended the workshop be fully aware that they would be participating in research and not a traditional conference session. IRB required us to submit our official session description to them for review and that it include language identifying it as a research study. We were required to use that description in all conference materials such as the Social Work Day program.

Marketing

We also presented a brief overview of our work at Social Work Day's opening plenary, and circulated flyers and recruitment materials around the conference. We created postcards with our IRB approved session description and distributed them to those arriving at Social Work Day. Additionally, in the weeks leading up to ICQI, our workshop description was shared through the Social Work Day listserv.

Our research questions focused on social work scholars; so our recruitment efforts were focused on Social Work Day, rather than across ICQI. We got positive feedback among those we spoke with, though the busy nature of conferences made it so that not all who would have liked to attend the workshop were able to. Some elected to do an interview instead.

Social Work Day provided an invigorating and affirming environment and offered the perfect "home-base" for our research. It allowed us to collect data through rich dialogues and interactive activities including engaging participants in preliminary data analysis of the experiences they shared with each other.

A Global Sample

We are grateful to our workshop and interview participants who came from across the United States and some from other countries. Though we are in the early stages of data analysis, we are finding that we have many experiences in common. Participants spoke about the transformative power of qualitative work and PAR/CBPR and their commitment to methodologies that serve to generate knowledge and address complex social issues in new ways.

However, PAR and CBPR are time intensive and involve co-researching with individuals outside academia. This can present many logistical and ethical challenges, which were also shared across those who participated. For example, obtaining IRB approval, balancing multiple conflicting needs such as the demands of academic publishing and the desires and goals of your co-researchers, as well as building new relationships when you arrive to a community as a doctoral student or faculty member.

Why Do PAR/CBPR?

A commitment to doing research with rather than on and social work values like social justice were some reasons offered for how participants persist, though our continued analysis will offer deeper understandings. As emerging scholars, facilitating this workshop was a rewarding experience, one that will inform our ongoing research agendas.

Our hope is that what we are learning from the workshop and interviews will provide new opportunities to generate conversation among social work scholars and practitioners, and potentially offer new pathways forward for greater use of PAR/CBPR and related methodologies in social work.

Isolation & Detachment

Many shared feelings of being isolated and detached from a social work community doing similar research. Offering our workshop at Social Work Day and collecting data on site in creative and collaborative ways was a step toward building such a community as many realized others struggled with the same issues. We hope our research will continue to build community by sparking conversations and highlighting the shared experiences among those committed to participatory research methodologies.

Since ICQI, we have conducted additional interviews and have a second data-collection workshop planned this fall through connections made at Social Work Day. We are planning a series of publications on our findings and want to bring this work back to Social Work Day at ICQI in 2019.

Creating a Community
of Qualitative Inquiry

Austin Oswald
City University of New York, NY, USA
aoswald@gradcenter.cuny.edu

Attending Social Work Day was a profound moment in my academic career and an experience that I will never forget. As a first- time attendee,  I was honored to be a plenary speaker for the opening session on Social Work and the Common Good and, later in the day, to present my paper, Complex Intimacy: Theorizing Older Gay Men's Social Lives.

The Opening Plenary

The day started strong. At the opening plenary, I sat alongside a panel of three remarkable scholars and shared stories about navigating the complexities of our lived experiences and subjectivities. I was impressed by my colleagues' high level of reflexivity and the degree to which they subjected themselves to the same level of cultural analysis as they applied to their participants. Christine Mayors' talk about her intersecting identities, Burcu Ozturk's reflections as an immigrant student and her desire to improve the experiences of other immigrants, and Anindita Bhattacharya's remarks about being a feminist researcher in India's patriarchal culture were inspiring and caused me to think more deeply about my own social positions and the intended outcomes of my research.

Social Work Day exposed me to a community of qualitative social work researchers that I was desperately searching for. In the first year of my PhD studies, I completed four quantitative research courses and not a single qualitative course. I was beginning to wonder where all the qualitative social work researchers were.

I left Social Work Day feeling connected to a community of scholars that I did not have before. Events such as these are important for social work and to emerging scholars who might not otherwise have the opportunity to connect with a diverse group of qualitative researchers.

What's Next?

I am an editor of this newsletter for students and new professionals. I hope my tasks in this job keep me connected and allow me to support emerging scholars share their perspectives with the global *QISW* community.

I am grateful for Jane Gilgun's exceptional organizing skills, for the contributors to this newsletter, the establishment of the Social Work Day listserv, and the qualitative social work special interest groups. I look forward to staying connected throughout the year. See you at the eighth annual Social Work Day 15th annual International Congress of Qualitative Inquiry.

Drama Therapy & Social Work:
Social Work Day as an Adventure

Christine Mayor
Wilfrid Laurier University, Ontario, Canada
mayo6830@mylaurier.ca

Trained as a drama therapist and currently a social work PhD student, I had the freedom to present two very different kinds of work at Social Work Day. In the first, entitled Embodied Tableaux: Drama-Based Arts Based Research Methodology in Social Work Research, I demonstrated how an adapted drama therapy technique might work as a research method for social work.

In the second, entitled Teachers, Trauma, and the Classroom: Investigating Trauma Training for Working with Syrian Refugee Students, I presented thematic analysis of interviews focusing on trauma training with teachers who are working with Syrian refugee students. In both, I briefly discussed how my cross training in social work and drama therapy helped me understand my research from different perspectives.

Much to Reflect Upon

I was also given the opportunity as an invited speaker at the opening plenary of Social Work Day to discuss how my personal and professional identities influence how I see the world and my future research. Here, I reflected on how it was perhaps unsurprising that I find myself attempting to negotiate between two disciplines and am looking for my epistemological and methodological home. I grew up in a bi-cultural family, with one parent from the Caribbean and one from Canada. Bermuda is my home, but I have now spent almost as many years living off the island as I have on it.

I have had full access to the benefits of white supremacy and white privilege, but my experiences growing up in my family and in Bermuda differ than many white Canadians. My early experiences with identity, geography, relationships, race, and culture continue to show up in my in-between-ness and professional interests.

Immersion in Practice

I have spent the last decade immersed in a clinical and community practice that sees the arts as a way of knowing and a method for social activism and healing. Within a drama therapy framework, I am used to engaging with the mind-body, affect, imagery, metaphor, story, roles, relationships, and improvisation in both research and practice. It is impossible to separate my drama therapy training from my qualitative research.

I also chose to return to school to pursue a PhD in social work because I felt the tools available to me in drama therapy were essential, but perhaps not sufficient to answer some of the questions I had about trauma, racialization, and the education system. Engaging in a social work doctoral program has pushed me to consider alternative ways of knowing, theorizing and researching.

Being brought into a new discipline has made me equal parts excited and concerned about what I am being asked to adopt. Straddling multiple perspectives, my first Social Work Day at ICQI was an adventure of attempting to imagine what an integrated qualitative research practice could be.

Political Neo-Pragmatism

During my first PhD course, I was introduced to Gibson's (2010) conceptualization of "political neo-pragmatism," which has been deeply helpful in my process of defining my approach to qualitative research. As she articulates, this epistemology combines: (1) political responsibility through a commitment to social justice, (2) ethical considerations of the impact of our research and how it is disseminated, and (3) epistemological and methodological flexibility in order to best serve the needs of individuals and communities. She keeps her sight on her audience as she speaks, remembering both what gets lost or is at risk in making certain concessions, but also what might be at risk if she does not make these strategic choices.

I am interested in how this body and mind shapes how I see a problem, what questions I ask, what kinds of data I elicit, how I analyze data, and how I share my findings. I used[CM3] these perspectives in the two presentations shared at Social Work Day. During the plenary panel, I also considered how these perspectives might influence my future research.

Whiteness & Trauma

Indeed, my future dissertation work focuses on how whiteness is interwoven with foundational assumptions about trauma, particularly in the educational system. My personal experiences with whiteness, working as a trauma therapist, and working in schools as both a therapist and as an educator implicate me deeply in the work. I imagine I will continue to draw on both my drama therapy and social work training throughout the various stages of my dissertation project.

I am grateful for the questions and engagement with these ideas at Social Work Day, which have strengthened my drive to work through how I bring my whole self to a project. I feel inspired by courageous discussions that critically examined the role of social work in legacies of harm and our own responsibilities in doing research. Finally, I look forward to continuing to question how to balance political necessity, aesthetic imaginings, and relational ethics in research in our future gatherings together.

Citation

Gibson, M. (2010). Building research, building justice: Epistemology, social work, and lesbian parents. *Canadian Social Work Review, 27(2)*, 239-258.

Art-Based Research & Theatre of the Oppressed

M. Candace Christensen
University of Texas San Antonio, USA
Candace.Christensen@utsa.edu

In 2009, I started working on my dissertation research which was comprised of using theatre of the oppressed (TO) methodology to develop, implement, and evaluate a campus sexual assault prevention program. At that time, I only found one social work scholar who had conducted a similar project. In the years since, I have witnessed a growing interest in TO methodology within academic social work circles. I entered into Social Work Day 2018 with the intent to locate other researchers interested in TO methodology. My aim is to build a network of social work scholars interested in arts-based research (ABR), particularly TO.

During the opening plenary, I was excited to hear that Christine Mayor had a background in drama therapy. I made note to attend her presentation later in the day. Listening to the doctoral students describe their specific research interests gave me a snapshot of where the next wave of qualitative social work research is heading.

While attending Christine's presentation, I took copious notes on the embodied tableaux methodology, which she illustrated. The methods involve participants in developing visual stories with their bodies. The researcher photographs the tableaux and asks the participants discuss how and why they developed the tableaux.

Making Connections

Christine's research inspired me to use this methodology in a future project. I spoke with Christine after the session and asked how I can find details on the methodology she developed. It was so much fun to talk with another theatre person. Like me, Christine was expressive; She used her face and body to communicate, as much as words. I plan on staying in contact with Christine about potential future collaborations.

More Arts-Based Research

I attended another afternoon presentation that showcased several different ABR methods. I was particularly struck by the interpretive phenomenological analysis method presentation by Sarah Vicary. The method involves participants in drawing pictures that capture the essence of the topic under investigation. I can see how the pictures illuminate a way of perceiving that is emotional, symbolic, and corporeal. This is another method I would like to use in the future.

I wrapped up the day by attending the closing plenary where we engaged in a group discussion about our individual and collective experiences with the day. I left Social Work Day 2018 feeling assured and inspired by the ABR presentations I witnessed. I felt assured that ABR has a home in social work scholarship, and I felt inspired to use new ABR methods and develop collaborations. Back to ToC

Unheard Stories of Survivors of Intimate Partner Violence Among Immigrant Families in the United States

Burcu Ozturk
University of Alabama, Tuscaloosa, USA
bozturk@crimson.ua.edu

I was one of four PhD students who presented at the opening plenary of Social Work Day 2018. The topic was Social Work and the Common

Good. The description of the plenary noted that social work has a common vision while welcoming multiple perspectives. Our task as presenters was to answer four questions: what social locations do I occupy? Why is my research important? What impact do I want my research to have? What do I do to ensure that my research has impact? After their presentation, participants will share their own visions for their research.

Social Location

I am a doctoral student at the University of Alabama, Tuscaloosa. I have been living in the United States for almost six years. I came to the United States to obtain my masters and PhD degrees via a Turkish government scholarship. The plan is for me to return to Turkey and become a university professor in social work. My research is on intimate partner violence among Middle Eastern female survivors in the United States. Although I do not have direct experience with intimate partner violence in my personal life, I know the stories from my friends and relatives. I have witnessed conflict and violent relationships among couples I know. I also did a one-month internship as a group counselor for battered women during my undergraduate studies in social work in Turkey. It was hard and heartbreaking to witness the effects of violence and not be able to do anything for the survivors.

Importance of my Research

The participants in the group shared their stories with me and other women. Many of did not know about government resources such as health care and education. They suffered abuse from their husbands who spent money on drinking and left the women to care for the families alone. These women wished that their husbands would find good jobs and help them. These issues also affected their children who began to develop behavioral problems. As a result of seeing these domestic and social problems I decided to study intimate partner violence.

My topic for my dissertation research is unheard stories of survivors of intimate partner violence in immigrant
families in the United States. My research focuses on Middle Eastern immigrant female survivors in the United States. There is a worldwide 35% prevalence rate of women as having experienced intimate partner violence (WHO, 2013). Many of them not only survive physical violence, but also experience rape and emotional abuse.

More Than 40 Million Refugees

As we see the dynamic changes in the world, refugees and immigrant populations have been increasing year by year. The record shows that 43.2 million immigrants lived in the U.S. in 2015 (Lopez& Radford, 2017) and specifically 1.2 million immigrants from Middle East and North Africa are in the U.S. (Migration Policy Institute, 2017). When immigrants move to other countries, they encounter language barriers, adaptation issues in terms of culturally-bound expectations, financial difficulties, isolation, and issues related to immigration statues. Those are the reasons that immigrants and refugees are among the more vulnerable populations in the United States.

I am using intersectionality theory in my research. This theory allows social workers to analyze the oppressions faced by women, especially nonwhite women, in the United States. The fundamental insight from intersectionality theory involves observation of how social categories, by which hierarchies of power and opportunities are formed, affects individuals (Marecek, 2016).

Intersectionality

Intersectional analysis illuminates the intensification of women's oppression and the effects of discrimination through the categories of race, ethnicity, class, gender, sexual orientation, and immigrant status (Marecek, 2016). Understanding the intersectionality of race, class, gender, marginalization, oppression and discrimination and how the intersections influence domestic violence in the lives of immigrant women will deepening understandings of issues that confront immigrant women and their families (Sokoloff, 2008).

My goal is that my research will expose and bring into the open those unheard voices in society. I want to tell their stories, and I hope those stories will help affect policy making. I assume those women have language barriers, health insurance issues, and difficulties to adapt their self in the culture. So this study can bring their obstacles to the professional literature, enabling social workers, domestic violence against women providers, and policy makers to use the knowledge my study will provide when they implement interventions and empowerment programs for those survivors. For my study, I will do qualitative study to explore their stories. I believe that qualitative research will provide rich and comprehensive pictures of the survivors' lives. Intersectionality theory provides the theoretical perspectives that will aid my analysis, interpretation, and dissemination of findings.

Ensuring Impact

I am taking steps to ensure my research has impact. One step is conference presentations. At Social Work Day, I not only presented in this plenary, but I also was a panel member on a session entitled Intersectionality and Women's Experience. With my dissertation advisor, Debra Nelson-Gardell, we implemented an interactive session that invited those who attended the session to contribute their personal and professional experiences with intimate partner violence. The feedback for this interactive sessions was positive with participants stating how much they learned through this experiential and theoretically-informed approach. In addition, a video of my plenary presentation is available on YouTube at https://www.youtube.com/edit?o=U&video_id=epdM-V1LNf .

Finally, I have written this article for *Qualitative Inquiry in Social Work* (*QISW*). I hope that being the editor for Eastern Europe for *QISW* will bring wide attention to intimate partner violence among refugee families. This position will also allow me to solicit articles about intimate partner violence for *QISW* as well as other topics, too. Back to ToC

Citations

Sokoloff, N. J. (2008). Expanding the intersectional paradigm to better understand domestic violence in immigrant communities. *Critical Criminology, 16(4),* 229.

Marecek, J. (2016). Invited reflection: Intersectionality theory and feminist psychology. *Psychology of Women Quarterly, 40(2),* 177-181.

Lopez, G., Radford, J. (2017). Facts on U.S. Immigrants, 2015: Statistical portrait of the foreign-born population in the United States. Pew Research Hispanic Center, Washington, DC (2017).

World Health Organization. (2013). *Global and regional estimates of violence against women: prevalence and health effects of intimate partner violence and non-*

partner sexual violence. 2013, 57. http://doi.org/10.1007/s13398-014-0173-7.2

Migration Policy Institute (2018). *Middle East and North African Immigrants in the United States.* Retrieved from: https://www.migrationpolicy.org/article/middle-eastern-and-north-african-immigrants-united-states

Pride, Relationships, and Generosity
at Social Work Day and ICQI

Debra Nelson-Gardell
University of Alabama, Tuscaloosa, USA
dnelsong@sw.ua.edu

My professional identity focuses on social work, even though I also teach, research, and serve as an academic. My first identity is that of social worker,  rather than "faculty member," which some might expect. Perhaps many social work faculty fault those academics who see themselves as social workers first, academics second? I actively choose to privilege social worker in my identity. Perhaps because of that, my joy anticipating, experiencing, then reflecting on the content that a social worker delivered as one of the ICQI keynote speeches influenced my entire ICQI experience, including Social Work Day. My pride in anticipating and then watching a social worker, Dr. Karen Staller, in front of a group of intellectuals I admire, respect, and value swelled my heart (https://goo.gl/p1FhoZ).

Relationships

The relationship aspect of ICQI Social Work Day stands out for me. I experienced acceptance, warmth, intellectual challenge, and heartening. And because of that, I experience gratitude. ICQI makes me feel special, not less than.

Generosity

The intellectual generosity of workshop attendees at my student's and my presentation took me aback for a moment. Burcu asked our workshop attendees to offer suggestions, voice their concerns, and identify issues she should consider as she embarks upon her dissertation research project. The outpouring overwhelmed us both. She realized the importance of her work. I realized (yet again) the value of multiple brains working in unison. For a moment, I feared judgement—that those in attendance would wonder at my competence (or lack thereof) related to my abilities to mentor a doctoral researcher. Then, I realized that in seeking help, in seeking others' intellectual input, I was indeed mentoring. I wrote a haiku in response to my experiences.

My ICQI.
Renewal, relationships.
Enriched learning shared.

The Audacity to Hope:
Liberation from a Cloistered Space

Freda V. Coleman-Reed
University of North Alabama, Florence, USA
fvcolemanreed@una.edu

I brought to Social Work Day the audacity to hope. Hope for what? I hoped for liberation from my cloistered academic space through immersion and exposure to qualitative inquiry approaches and perspectives. I hoped to embrace discourse on qualitative inquiry that enhanced my teaching of social work education as well as social work practice.

In truth, I arrived at ICQI with an air of hesitancy, yet expectancy. Also, I brought with me uncertainty about how this experience could better align my teaching of social work to useful and effective application in professional social work practice settings for my students. I did not anticipate I would encounter fellow Social Worker educators and practitioners grappling with similar thoughts and feelings.

Hesitant & Expectant

Traveling from my accommodations to Social Work Day in a shuttle bus, I struck-up a conversation with another social work educator who shared similar concerns and hopes. Our casual conversation evolved into a review of our, respective, academic years. Initially, it appeared we had different experience. They would prove to be very similar.

From more than 10 years of teaching, I shared concerns about an increasing emphasis on research and publication at my, heretofore, teaching-focused institution. While understanding the importance of research, I experienced the spoken and unspoken institutional shift as frustrating, distracting, and distancing from meaningful education and mentoring of future social workers. I found myself often struggling to serve two masters, my responsibility to the profession of social work (my students) and my responsibility to the institution.

By contrast, my fellow traveler discussed disillusionment, discomfort, and cognitive dissonance felt in his first year teaching social work at a research-intensive institution. He loved teaching his students, but struggled with making his teaching meaningful. He felt burdened with executing research demands and questioned the relevance of his research to social work. Removing our seeming differences, we had similar questions. How can we be effective social work educators and practitioners who are faithful to the mission of social work? Have we lost our way?

During our conversation, he had a sparkle in his eye and a brilliant smile which was contagious. It contrasted with the experiences he related of feeling drained and disconnected from social work practice. Was this why he had completed his PhD to be disconnected from the very things that he loved about social work?

That question resonated with me in my own review of the academic year. We discovered in our musings, we had similar thoughts and experiences that brought us to this moment in time we found ourselves in. As life would have it, at two different places, we received information that would lead us to ICQI and Social Work Day. His co-worker and my mentor, Debra Nelson-Gardell at the University of Alabama, independent of each other, offered encouragement to us to attend ICQI. Debra an exemplary educator, researcher, clinician, and all around great human being!

These independent conversations both suggested what we both loved about social work could be re-ignited at Social Work Day and ICQI: connection to people, commitment to social change, pursuit of social justice, and re-affirmation about the power of social work education and practice. By the time we reached the Congress, I noticed a growing feeling of anticipation about what was to come.

Uncertainty & Hope

Stepping from the shuttle, I retained a dose of uncertainty, but, I held out hope Social Work Day could be a vehicle for positive change in my teaching, research, and scholarship. Hope validated by my most recent conversation and emanating from observations made to me by my mentor prior to the Congress. I could hear my mentor describing the Congress, in particular Social Work Day, as a space that refreshes and renews academicians for teaching, research, and the practice of social work. My first time attending Social Work Day did not disappoint.

Once through the Congress doors, I was immediately enveloped in a sea of helping-kind. All around me an atmosphere full of hope urgency, expectancy, collegiality, and earnest inquiry abounded. For some, there appeared to be an air of uncertainty similar to what I brought in with me to the space. Listening to those around me, I heard dialogues that pushed against the bounds that tether social worker educators as well as practitioners. I overheard one social work educator/ researcher state to another colleague, "I'm so excited about the various discussions about research methods. I thinking about adding photovoice as an approach in my research methods course to create a richer experience for students and research participants!" I thought, "Me, too!"

Social Work Day challenged participants to operate beyond a prescribed or contrived lens of the academic and practice world. It encouraged me and other participants to collaborate, empower, advocate, and seek more knowledge and understanding of the others' experiences.

In that space, freedom to explore and express outside of rigidly contrived bounds was fully embraced. I came seeking hope and found I was challenged to make classroom social work education relevant and applicable to "real world" social work practice. It echoed in areas of the room and small group gatherings. The cacophony of sound and ideas provided affirmation for me that others struggle with making meaningful bridges for student social workers from the academic environment to social work practice. While this is somewhat disorienting, challenging, and exciting for me, I felt validated.

Connections to Colleagues

I felt emboldened to make connections with others present and create think space opportunities to address some of challenges I brought to Social Work Day and ICQI. I'm normally hesitant to launch into discourse with strangers about issues of the day and how social workers can and should make a difference.

When provocative or stimulating points resonated with me were made, I found myself freely talking with others about topics such as social justice for incarcerated populations, the differing experiences of people of color in privilege spaces, and the natural fit of qualitative inquiry to investigate and explicate social work practice.

Empowerment

As a social worker, I'm trained to empower people within their social contexts, but I hadn't meaningfully sought what I readily offer to others. I, also, understand social work as a profession predicated on empowerment, giving a voice to the voiceless, marginalized, and the oppressed. Social Work Day took me to the core focus of social work and connected me to colleagues who had similar challenges and pursuits. It afforded me the opportunity to take in new, different, and varied approaches to the issues important to the profession of social work and social workers: vulnerable populations, poverty, immigration, human rights, economic and social injustice.

Marx (2014) stated, "Social work has survived as a profession in part because of its broad applicability in an ever-changing world (p. 84)." I suspect social workers like myself, and others, have survived and thrived in the profession because we have gathered together and shared our experiences as social workers. It is empowering to meet with other social workers who understand the varied experiences of social, economic, and political injustice that we are charged to addressed as a profession. It, also, affords us an opportunity to come together to generate ideas and initiatives to individually as well as collectively respond. It provides a space for social work education and practice to join together in those efforts.

Social Work Spaces

I suspect changes in the social work profession occur at times and in spaces were social workers can feely dialogue, generate ideas, spark creative, and empower each other to new action. This occurs in spaces similar to Social Work Day at ICQI. By the end of Social Work Day, I felt a crack had occurred in my previously cloistered academic experience. Social Work Day and ICQI offered intellectual stimulation, development of new collegial relationships, and invigorating professional discourse.

My views had expanded, and I was overflowing with qualitative research ideas. I'd taken steps to join with others to explore new research opportunities directly related to practice. I left Social Work Day with questions to answer over the next year: How can I continue to take advantage of this moment in time to empower myself? How can I make what I teach transmit the rich and dynamic profession of social work? How can I use qualitative inquiry as a useful vehicle to assist with the social work students understanding and preparation for "real world" social work practice?

Social Work Day as Empowering

Finally, social work aims to create avenues to empower individuals, groups, organizations, and systems; while reducing barriers and equipping people to obtain needed resources, benefits, and services to meet life task (Germaine & Gitterman, 1995). This happened for me as a social worker at Social Work Day. I was empowered, barriers percieved as limiting were reduced or reframed, resources were obtained, and I was equipped with a new group of colleagues to meet my academic and professional task. I left refreshed and renewed for teaching, research, and the practice of social work. My experiences and resolves from Social Work Day brought to mind a poem by Guilliame Appollinaire that I often quoted during my sojourn through my PhD program.

Come to the edge," [s]he said.

They said, "We are afraid"
"Come to the edge," [s]he said
They came
[S]he pushed them... and they flew.

I left Social Work Day flying! I look forward to what next year's Social Work Day brings.

Citations

Appollinaire, Guillaume (2015). *Zone: Selected poems* (R. Padgett, Translator). New York, NY: New York Review of Books.

Germaine, Carol B., & Gitterman, Alex (1995). Ecological Perspective. In R.L. Edwards (Ed.), *The Encyclopedia of Social Work* (19th ed.) pp. 816-824). Silver Spring, MD: National Association of Social Workers.

Marx, Jerry D. (2014). Ten emerging "communities" for social work education and practice. *Social Work, 59(1)*, 84-86. doi:10.1093/sw/swt042 Back to ToC

Drawing and IPA for Social Work Research

Sarah Vicary
Open University, Milton, Keynes, UK
sarah.vicary@open.ac.uk

I was delighted to have my paper accepted for Social Work Day at ICQI and welcomed the opportunity to share my latest work with colleagues in America and beyond. In summary, the paper I presented concerned the use of drawing as a way of undertaking research in social work and also a plea for this research community to consider using interpretative phenomenological analysis (IPA) (Smith et al, 2009), both for me are a great fit.

Exploring Meanings

Drawing is used as a data generation tool in many areas of research including social work because it uses different cognitive processes. Drawing also provides an opportunity for researchers to access thoughts, feelings and emotions in different ways. In IPA, imaginative methods that allow such discovery, are encouraged. In the study which was the focus of my paper, one drawing method, rich pictures (Checkland, 1981), was used in order to evoke thoughts and feelings in a way unfamiliar to participants, thereby allowing an opportunity to explore meaning that might otherwise be hidden.

IPA was applied to verbatim texts that included the description of the participant's rich picture which were utilised, either whole or in part, to illustrate the findings. The rationale for its use in generating data I have discussed more fully elsewhere under my previous name (Matthews, 2013). The paper for this conference discussed whether, for IPA, drawing can be used to elicit and illustrate data in troubled times. The troubled times concern the independent review of mental health legislation in England and Wales and the impact this may bring for social workers.

New Connections

The conference did not disappoint! I had many enjoyable conversations and now the beginnings of new connections through this group and publications such as this. I was also able to attend a range of other seminars and in particular was keen to hear more about the use of qualitative software tools for data management in which I developed a real interest, despite my previous lack of affinity with most things technical. You can find my latest paper on this subject through my staff profile below (Vicary et al, 2017).

I very much look forward to extending the reach of this group throughout the United Kingdom.

Sources

Checkland, Peter B. (1981). *Systems thinking, systems practice.* London: Wiley

Matthews, Sarah. (2013). *Using drawing to generate data: Exploring the role and experiences of Approved Mental Health Professionals.* Sage Research Case Methods. London: Sage.

Smith, Johnathon. A., Flowers, Paul, & Larkin, Michael (2009) *Interpretative phenomenological analysis: Theory, method, research.* London: Sage

Vicary, Sarah, Young, Alys, & Hicks, Stephen (2017). A reflective journal as learning process and contribution to quality and validity in Interpretative Phenomenological Analysis. *Qualitative Social Work 16(4),* 550-565

What's in a Name? Thematic Analyses as we Know Them

Beth Archer-Kuhn
University of Calgary, Canada
beth.archerkuhn@ucalgary.ca

Thematic analysis may not be what you think. "van Manen's thematic analysis is used in phenomenology. It's not Braun and Clarke (2006)," I hear myself saying with confidence. And so it begins; my first open dialogue at Social Work Day, comparing thematic analyses. I am excited to be here with peers, yet unknown to me, to engage in dialogue about these two different analytic methods.

A Step-by-Step Approach

Popular in studies is the use of Braun and Clarke (2006) wherein the writer highlights for the reader in a very systematic way how themes emerge from the narrative, transforming the raw data of multiple transcripts through six steps of codes to themes to sub-themes: 1) familiarising yourself with your data; 2) generating initial codes; 3) searching for themes; 4) reviewing themes; 5) defining and naming themes; and, 6) producing the report. Direct quotes are used to illustrate the meaning of the themes and sub-themes from the participant reflections on their experience. This is the known, the familiar, the acceptable. Yet, I am introducing another way.

Studying the audience carefully, I observe their blank faces as I reveal thematic analysis as described by van Manen (2017): 1) identify lived experience description (LED); 2) create an anecdote; 3) reflect on the anecdote; 4) create wonder about the phenomenon using literature; and, 5) lift up the phenomena to reveal its uniqueness. The LED provides the concreteness of the experience of one participant. Direct quotes from participant illuminate reflection in the experience.

I share a small snippet of a participant quote, an LED to illustrate a theme; pressure of the invisibility, accountability debate, using the process described by van Manen (2014). The participant in this study, a child welfare worker, reveals the concrete, in the moment experience, and the sense of anxiety with the awareness of current practices that render mom's accountable and dad's invisible, as she listens to discussions in a professional development training that link masculinity and domestic violence. Reflection in the experience provides greater insight into the worker experience.

Anxiety rises from my tummy to my neck. Flittering butterflies now feel heavy and solid, a lump in my throat and I can't breathe with the naked awareness; where is dad in our case note? In our files? How do we protect this little one? Frustration propels me with all the attention on mom, yet I sense a long road ahead.

van Manen's (1998/2007) considers phenomenology as both a description and interpretation of the lived experience. He posits that phenomenology is always re-evoking the experience, exploring what is given in the moment (van Manen, 2014). To do this requires the researcher to maintain a curiosity or wonder about the phenomena as they appear, focusing on meanings from their origins, known as reduction. Reduction in phenomenology is achieved through two critical components, epoche or bracketing and the reduction proper or reflective phenomenological attitude that allows phenomenon to show itself (van Manen, 2014).

According to van Manen (2017) when we look at something phenomenologically, we lift it up and wonder, what is this experience like? Epoche means bracketing that which we previously knew so that we might be open to the phenomenon, while reduction refers to understanding a phenomenon from its origins, as it shows itself to our consciousness, rather than how we understand it based on our previous knowledge (van Manen, 2014). Still, the two tenets of phenomenology work together to reveal lived experience. Bracketing involves remaining open to phenomenological meanings through lived experience descriptions that move through multiple layers of thematic analysis (van Manen, 2014).

Meaning Making

It is Social Work Day today and the audience can appreciate the pressures experienced by child welfare workers who have to face daily demands of domestic violence work. The audience is curious, asking challenging and meaningful questions and sharing their understandings of thematic analysis, as we reflect on and make meaning together. They too are drawn in to the collaborative nature afforded by this open, inviting annual conference.

Citations

Braun, V., & Clarke, V. (2006). Using thematic analysis in psychology. *Qualitative Research in Psychology, 3*, 77-101.

van Manen, M. (2017). *Phenomenology in its original sense.* Unpublished manuscript.

van Manen, M. (2014). *Phenomenology of practice: Meaning-giving methods in Phenomenological Research and Writing* (Vol. 13). New York: Left Coast Press.

van Manen, M. (1998/2007). *Researching Lived Experience. Human Science for an Action- Sensitive Pedagogy.* London, ON: Althouse Press.

An Opportunity to Reflect, Experience, and Meet

Guy Enosh
University of Haifa, Israel
enosh@research.haifa.ac.il

When I sat down to write this small piece, I didn't realize how difficult it will turn out to be, and what a slalom of self-reflectivity it would take me.  So this piece is in a way, may be referred to as an ethno-methodology… or if you prefer, a personal narrative encompassing a twelve-year process.

A Confession

In this vein, I will start with a confession. I first attended ICQI the first year it was announced, twelve years ago. I was thrilled. I was looking so much to find out about new methods of qualitative research, new avenues of research, and meet like-minded scholars. Norman Denzin was a "childhood" hero for me. I grew up through my days in my master degree reading his books.

I was always interested in methodology and different methodological developments and approaches. Methodology for me indicates a way of thinking, a way of approaching the world, of constructing knowledge. Different methodologies, be they quantitative or qualitative, are different ways of thinking, of constructing models of the world we live in and encounter.

I expected the ICQI to offer me an opportunity to experience new methodological approaches and to have lively discussions regarding new ways of thinking. However, (and this is me, my limitations), I encountered at this first meeting a new methodology, which I experienced as too far-out, a methodology which was not a methodology as I understood the term – "performing auto-ethnography". I attended sessions that looked like interesting performances, some better, some worse – but where was the methodology? The raising of meaning from concrete findings/knowledge/experience to a more abstract understanding?

Where Were Social Workers?

What I missed mostly there was meeting social workers and the opportunity to share ideas, research interests and application of research methods to social work relevant subjects.

For the following seven years, I avoided the conference.

On the other hand, I tended to go on a regular basis to the Society for Social Work and Research (SSWR) conference. Although it was heavily biased towards quantitative methods and positivistic approaches, it opened opportunities to meet other social-work researchers with similar interests and other fascinating foci of research. However, although there are some qualitative meetings and presentations at the SSWR, something was missing.

Another Chance
Through the SSWR conference I met Jane and learned about the establishment of Social Work Day in ICQI. So I gave it a chance five years ago and have been attending on a regular basis since. For me, Social Work Day provides plenty of opportunities to meet other social workers, time for discussions, for testing and experiencing new modes of presentation and even learning more and gaining a better understanding of auto-ethnography... and trying my hand at it. For me it is a celebration of qualitative research in social work. And most important—an opportunity to reflect, experience, and meet. A place to grow in.

Friendly, Fortunate Forays into Social Work Day

Tamara H. Shetron
Texas State University, San Marcos, USA
tamarashetron@txstate.edu

I feel fortunate that my education research was included in the Social Work Day. In 2015, my first presentation with colleagues, Divergent Student  Conversations (2015), appeared as part of the regular qualitative conference. Subsequent presentations continuing the theme of student development in 2016 and 2017 appeared in Social Work Day. I questioned this placement at first, but upon reflection, this placement proved to be beneficial for deepening my thinking and helping me understand and appreciate the interconnectedness between social work and my field, developmental education.

Developmental Education

Developmental education is the study of academic, affective, social, and other supports needed to help nontraditional and/or underprepared college students succeed in higher education. Nontraditional students include first in families to attend college, non-English speakers, students from low socioeconomic backgrounds, students with children and jobs, veterans, and any student who may need additional support to succeed in their studies.

The research I brought to Social Work Day in 2016 was the second part of a three-year longitudinal study focused on the college student experiences of my own daughter, Nina Harper, who was a college freshman in 2014-2015. The first year (2015), my colleagues, Kristie O'Donnell-Lussier, Jodi Lampi and I presented a study that illuminated concepts of student development woven throughout the dystopian novel, Divergent by Veronica Roth.

Nina Joins the Study

My daughter, Nina, was a college freshman that year, and she agreed to be part of the study. I provided her with guiding prompts and asked her to keep a journal of her experiences during her freshman year. Having been a lifetime journal keeper, I still had an account of my own freshman year. This provided a mother/daughter comparison that we analyzed through student development lenses.

I could not have imagined at the time of our first presentation in 2015 what the next year would bring. During her sophomore year, Nina faced an unexpected pregnancy. In full mom mode, I continued our study thinking that it would help me provide a supportive framework for her and at the same time help alleviate some of the more potentially inflammatory mom-daughter dynamic.

Positive Outcomes

Using the study as a means of talking about her situation allowed us to focus on her continued growth and development and to assure her that what was happening to her in the moment did not define her as an individual or define her future. What I did not account for fully was the role social workers played in her ability to navigate the pregnancy and early motherhood.

In 2016, our study, Slow Cooking with Support Systems: Navigating College as a Single Parent, was included at Social Work Day. During that presentation (with baby in tow) it struck me fully that our story, and indeed, my daughter's continued healthy growth and development, was now due to the impact of social support services in her life. At this point, I saw how beautifully intertwined social services and education really were, particularly for individuals with extensive support needs.

Social Work as a New World

Being included in the Social Work Day opened my mind to a whole new world of possibilities for providing seamless support students for college students that are integrated with already established local, state, or federally funded programs. My own area of research, postsecondary education for students with intellectual disabilities, emphasizes the importance of establishing strong collaborations between social services and higher education and purposefully considers how public resources (such as vocational rehabilitation) can work with inclusive college education to provide the best continuing educational opportunities in socially valued (rather than segregated) locations.

Partnerships

Some colleges are creating partnerships with community organizations to help students facing food insecurity, and organizations such as Single Stop and the Center for Working Families attempt to coordinate existing social safety-net services and campuses are also hiring social workers. Unfortunately, though, many social safety nets exclude college students (Broton, & Goldrick-Rab, 2016). The integration of social services with other college student supports opens an important line of inquiry regarding the impact of such services. Questions such as the effect of social services on student success and retention, sense of belonging, and sense of well-being all come to mind.

Effective Supports

Creating research partnerships between social workers and college support professionals through qualitative inquiry of college student experience could become a driving force to creating more robust and supportive services and help equalize the higher education playing field for marginalized and underserved students.

Citation

Broton, K., & Goldrick-Rab, S. (2016). The dark side of college (un) affordability: Food and housing insecurity in higher education. *Change: The Magazine of Higher Learning, 48(1),* 16-25

Pop-Up Session on Race & Research

By Jane Gilgun
University of Minnesota, Twin Cities, USA
jgilgun@umn.edu

Tom Kenemore's discussion on race and research during the morning Round Robin sparked a pop-up session on race and research later in the day that Tom, Stephen Wilson, and I participated in. We videotaped it, and Sondra Vogel was the videographer. Jane and Tom had done research on young black men for decades. We are both white and older. Stephen is an African American clinical professor whose research is with young black men.

Relationships in Research

We discussed how we build relationships in research when race and racial stereotypes are in play. Tom has found it important to put issues on the table, but the timing of such discussions and how to put these often hidden issues on the table. Moral injury, shame and vulnerability as African American men were also part of the conversation. The sexualization of African American men that goes back to slavery was important part of the discussion. White people oiled down and displayed naked African American men on the slave block. Gender, age, and authority were also part of our discussion.

Videos

I made videos and put them on YouTube. The links are below.

Social Work Day 2018 Videos

At Social Work Day 2018, I videotaped two of the sessions and Sondra Vogel videotaped the pop-up session on race and research. Jane made the videotapes into movies. These are the movies and their links to YouTube.

Social Work for the Common Good, Part 1: Austin Oswald's Research on LGBT Elders
https://www.youtube.com/watch?v=-Cu_acBQIbg

Social Work for the Common Good, Part 2: Burcu Ozturk, Intimate Partner Violence in Immigrant Families in the US
https://www.youtube.com/watch?v=epdM-V1LNfI&t=106s

Social Work for the Common Good, Part 3: Anindita Bhattacharya, Forgotten Women in India
https://www.youtube.com/watch?v=_ErukdErAmA

Sondra Fogel on Translating Research Findings to Practice in Journal Articles
https://www.youtube.com/watch?v=_MD-MNpNVwU

Sondra Fogel on Language Issues in Academic Publishing
https://www.youtube.com/watch?v=LILPUHbV_kI

Jim Drisko Content Analysis in Social Work
https://youtu.be/P-ObJlJN2gc

Tom Kenemore on Race and Research
https://www.youtube.com/upload?redirect_to_classic=true

Narrative Research with Indigenous People in Chile. Vanessa Jara-Larbathé & César Puebla-Cisneros
https://www.youtube.com/edit?o=U&video_id=wKyslnMsFzU

Masculinities, Race, & Research: Stephen Wilson, Tom Kenemore, & Jane Gilgun
https://www.youtube.com/edit?video_referrer=watch&video_id=q8aDIjQ7puA

Shame, Race, & Research: Stephen Wilson, Tom Kenemore, & Jane Gilgun
https://www.youtube.com/edit?video_id=hkgohso8aOA&video_referrer=watch

Moral Injury & Sex Offenders: Stephen Wilson, Tom Kenemore, & Jane Gilgun
https://www.youtube.com/edit?o=U&video_id=bNsH-HfvAss

Reflections on Qualitative Inquiry

Inquiry: A Seeking or Request for Truth, Information, or Knowledge

Jim Drisko
Smith College, Northampton, MA, USA
jdrisko@smith.edu

At the 2018 International Congress of Qualitative Inquiry's Social Work Day, a room full of participants introduced themselves and described their  areas of interest. Despite living and working in countries across several continents, it was striking to me that almost all focused on qualitative research approaches and methods, from grounded theory to phenomenology to participatory action research. Qualitative research was mentioned over and over again–appropriately–but here we were at a conference for qualitative inquiry.

To me inquiry is a much broader and inclusive term than is research. Inquiry alone may not be what is required for tenure and promotion, but the spirit of curiosity, exploration, wonder, and thinking that I associate with inquiry seems to me much more attractive, and frankly, much more fun. Inquiry may, or may not be, quite the same as research.

I have been drawn to the International Congress of Qualitative Inquiry (ICQI) for its diversity and its range of ideas, methods, affects, policies, and purposes. As Congress organizer Norman Denzin said, "This is the cutting edge in qualitative work." I got my introductions to Indigenous ways of knowing, to many forms of performance research, and to many types and approaches to critical theories and studies by attending ICQI over the years.

My own work has been both applauded and severely challenged at ICQI. I have learned a lot about the possibilities and modes of "inquiry." So what is the difference between "research" and "inquiry?" Or is there any difference?

Social work education emphasizes research over the broader terms scholarship and inquiry. In CSWE's EPAS 2015, the word "inquiry" is found eight times. In seven of eight mentions, inquiry is part of the phrase "scientific inquiry" as if inquiry has no other application. Only in discussion of the implicit curriculum, or the content in which education is delivered, does inquiry stand alone, separate from science. "Research" appears 15 times in the EPAS text.

Inquiry & Social Work

In the recent Group for the Advancement of Doctoral Education (2013) Quality Guidelines for PhD Programs in Social Work, research is the primary objective of doctoral level education. The Guidelines state that "research skills, broadly defined, involve the systematic collection and analysis of data that shed light on research questions relevant to social work."

Starting in the 1990s, social work began an effort to enhance the profession's research profile and its access to large scale grant monies. The effort has been quite successful, leading to the creation of the Society for Social Work and Research and increases in grant money obtained by many large universities. Along with this effort, research has gained in prominence and status in social work education.

The effort has been so successful that in 2000 the "St Louis Group" of 29 deans of "research intensive institutions" (those with or aspiring to multiple millions of dollars of external research funding) was created. One of the groups' objectives is to provide "a forum for deans, directors, and chairs to discuss problems and opportunities for the advancement of social work research." In 2009, the American Academy of Social Work and Social Welfare was announced. "The Academy is an honorific society of distinguished scholars and practitioners dedicated to achieving excellence in the field of social work and social welfare through high-impact work that advances social good."

Small Representation of Qualitative Inquiry

This "honorific" group has no clear membership criteria and is largely populated by social work researchers, very few of whom are known as qualitative researchers or inquirers. Yet the Academy has established and heavily promoted the "Grand Challenges" that shape several social work efforts and have served to delimit submissions to conferences of the social work membership organizations. Social work organizations heavily endorse research.

Scientific approaches to research, predominantly quantitative and probabilistic approaches, are promoted by EPAS standards and heavily taught in social work PhD programs. While EPAS standards have required education on qualitative methods since 1994, they are, in practice, minimally represented in MSW level courses and assignments. Similarly, just less than half of U.S. social work programs have any required course on qualitative research. Has inquiry been replaced by research?

The international Organization for Economic Cooperation and Development's Frascati Manual (2015), defines research "as creative and systematic work undertaken to increase the stock of knowledge, including knowledge of humans, culture and society, and the use of this stock of knowledge to devise new applications." Dictionary.com offers a more succinct definition: Research is the "diligent and systematic inquiry or investigation into a subject."

Research as Systematic

To me, research is the systematic study of a question or topic. It can be historical, a review of the literature, a systematic review, a synthesis of qualitative research, an exploratory study, a descriptive or correlational study, an experiment or RCT, or a qualitative study. There may be other types of research as well.

There does need to be a specific system that shapes the study--or perhaps more than one system (if the researcher is very good and very, very careful). Research requires a system, it is not piecemeal or made up as one goes.

To me, research is based on empirical knowledge. By empirical I mean "known through the senses" rather than conceptual, theoretical, value driven or imaginary without specific linkage to observable events. By empirical I do not solely mean "quantitative" or "using measurement techniques," though my students (often from psychology) have frequently been educated or socialized to think of "empirical" this way.

It is easy to think of research as being based on newly collected, or original, data. Yet, research may also be based on secondary data sets, a set of documents, a set of articles, or set of articles, chapters, books. Heinemann Pieper observed that articles, chapters, and books in fact make up an observable, empirical, data set which others may affirm, question or challenge. Perhaps we could say the same about ideas and concepts.

To me, research includes an obligation to seek out potentially disconfirming information or information that challenges and potentially alters or expands what we know about the question or topic. This obligation avoids the trap of simply lining up evidence that supports the researcher's preconceived (conscious, or unconscious or implicit) expectations. As Firebaugh states, "research should always have the potential for surprise."

Social Work Research

In social work, good research adds to knowledge of theory, or policy, or practice. Good research also adds to knowledge that can increase social justice; support physical, mental and social well-being; and allows people to realize their potential, cope effectively with life stresses, work productively, and contribute to their communities (after the World Health Organization's 2011 definitions of health and mental health). Good research should address both the "so what?" and "who cares?" questions fully.

What is Inquiry?

To me, inquiry has a much broader realm. Inquiry, according to the Cambridge Dictionary, is the process of asking. This surely fits. Even better if we add asking without limits–empirical, conceptual, philosophical, practical, political, economic, or cultural. Inquiry should be a process without boundaries.

Dictionary.com states inquiry involves a seeking or request for truth, information, or knowledge. I'd add seeking perspective and perhaps seeking ways of understating or ways of knowing. Inquiry often is 'meta' to what is being examined. Inquiry often goes outside the usual boxes of knowledge, methods, and content. It is not limited to empirical knowledge, very purposefully.

Inquiry is curious, reflexive and reflective; often it is critical and challenging. Inquiry asks that we pursue more than Kuhn's "normal science;" that we question and wonder about what we do and think--and why we do it. Anything may be questioned.

Inquiry may contest or deconstruct rules, norms and limits. Inquiry may reflectively look back at ones' self and question and ponder. It is often embodied, though it may also be very abstract. Inquiry may also reflexively look at social and cultural norms, power dynamics and taken for granted way of knowing and being. It helps us look at the contexts in which we research and practice.

Inquiry need not be limited to or by empirical data. Yet inquiry, as it unfolds, should be directed by the inquirer to look for its limitations, biases and blind spots. Inquiry should seek out potentially disconfirming ways or practices. Inquiry should look for greater complexity and unforeseen complications. In these ways research and inquiry have much in common.

Inquiry in Social Work

In social work, inquiry should be directly or indirectly focused on adding to ways of understanding, knowing, and practicing that increase social justice; support physical, mental and social well-being; and allows people to realize their potential, cope effectively with life stresses, work productively and contribute to their communities. However, these benefits may be indirect. Sometimes inquiry meanders and does not initially or always have an obvious direct linkage to practice or policy. Yet inquiry in social work should address the 'so what' and 'who cares' questions.

I'm not so sure about inquiry seeking "truth," though I think it's a worthy goal. (Are there multiple realities or multiple truths? Is it really possible to know another? Is it morally correct for us to write about other's experiences? As a social worker I often speak for others as an advocate – at best with a prior discussion that has included the other authorizing me to do this. Even so, such practices are, for me, loaded with moral, personal, and professional ambiguity. Inquiry can be an unsettling burden even as it is useful.)

Inquiry

I hope social workers, social work educators, and their organizations, stay open to inquiry as much as we do to research. Inquiry is a larger enterprise than research. It helps us see the merits and the limitation of research and how we do it. Inquiry keeps us grounded in power, money, culture and politics. Inquiry invites us to question and challenge ourselves. Inquiry should remind us about how we limit and even deceive ourselves. Inquiry invites us to aspire and think big. We should go for it!

Unlearning, Improvising, & Sparks of Understanding: An American Participant Observer of Recovery after Domestic Violence in Germany

Amy Chanmugam
The University of Texas at San Antonio, USA
Amy.Chanmugam@UTSA.edu

Until last summer, my experiences in participant observation were limited. Fortunately, I wrote a proposal to the German Academic Exchange Services to do an ethnography, which allowed me to adapt after arrival when it hit me how little I understood about my topic in context. In hindsight, I realize I was planning to lean into my comfort zone with interviews. Instead, day one of my work in Germany showed me that I understood far, far less than I had imagined, and every day of the following six weeks was a day of unlearning, eventually with sparks of understanding mixed in.

Naturally I learned much about myself, in addition to my topic. Learning about myself peaked on a day late in my visit when I thought a key informant was taking me to observe a group of women developing a theater project, when it was actually improv, and I was part of the group! Definitely more participating than observing. I sang, stood on a chair, mimed with a partner, acted like an elephant. I learned that the sense of gratitude I felt for all that the informant was sharing with me was a stronger force than the self-consciousness and confusion I felt in that unexpected situation… if she was going to open up experiences for me, I could only reciprocate by diving in.

In the enthusiasm and haste of preparing my proposal, I thought a narrow focus would be optimal for me as an American conducting research in Germany for the first time (as a child, I spoke fluent German and attended school there in the 1970s and 1980s, but had not been back much since). My study was titled, "The Role of Shelter-Based Peer Support for Youth and Mothers Recovering from Domestic Violence," and focused on a setting, topic, and population I was familiar with from my US research.

Limiting Assumptions

Fortunately, it was clear at the beginning of my stay that shelters and the notion of peer support were quite different in the northern German state where I was based (while domestic violence dynamics seemed the same).

Ethnography allowed me to recover from my limiting assumptions and expand my antennae.

For example, I soon learned that "shelter-based" was a limiting concept for the three shelters where I spent time for several reasons: child and adult shelter "graduates" maintained connections with current residents and staff (e.g., as weekly field trip participants or as volunteers); shelter buildings were more integrated with surrounding residential neighborhoods than US shelters I've seen; and shelter programming created opportunities for community interactions for residents (e.g., I attended a community presentation where current and former youth shelter residents collaborated to educate newly arrived immigrant children and mothers about child rights in Germany). Relationships thus transcended the shelter, with boundaries that were more permeable with the outside community than I had observed in the US.

Flat Hierarchies

Another example of my limiting assumptions was that the "peer" role highlighted in my proposal was less distinguishable than anticipated in the shelters because of flat hierarchies, consensus-based decision-making, and involvement of program graduates. The people I spent my days with did not have terminology separating residents from staff, volunteers, interns, former residents, current residents, or me. Relationships fell into an integrated, reciprocal person-helping-person ethos and it would have been artificial to separately examine relationships among residents currently identifying themselves as recovering after domestic violence. Again, my work was saved by ethnography, with the ability to revise the paths of my inquiry, based on evolving learnings.

Discoveries Through Dialogue

My discoveries through conversations were similar, where following unexpected pathways led to areas I would not have predicted. My greatest learnings occurred in dialogue arising through the questions they asked me: What are fathers like in the US.? Are there shelters in the U.S.? What are they like? (Surprise that US shelters have time limits for women fleeing domestic violence.) How can women rebuild after domestic violence in just a couple of months? What is it like in public for women wearing hijabs? A pregnant woman: Would my child be a citizen if born in the US.? (Concerns that child will be stateless.) Youth: Why do so many people have guns in the US.? Are there really gangs everywhere? Is it scary there for boys?

Several illuminating conversations occurred over meals (all three shelters had communally prepared and eaten meals at least once weekly). Clearly most experienced the shelter space as a home, and integrated me as a guest and a curiosity – some seemed amazed that I came all the way from the US and was interested in their lives – and reciprocated the interest.

Embracing Serendipity

My greatest joy during this data collection period was being able to roll with serendipitous circumstances to allow the discovery process to unfold. Prior to arrival in Germany, I had only one connection to their shelter system--an email correspondent I had never met. Shortly before my arrival she invited me to a coalition meeting that every shelter in the state would be sending a representative to, scheduled for the first day of my project-- an excellent opportunity for entrée.

Foreshadowing the subsequent improv experience, I learned just before the meeting that the first hour of their agenda was ME. My jet lag provided a feeling of intoxication that boosted my rusty conversational German, and allowed me to jump into dialogue about women's well-being in the US and Germany, colored by unknowns around the inauguration of President Trump five months earlier. It was a moment in time since past, after the election of the president despite his recorded comments about women on the Access Hollywood tapes, yet prior to the #MeToo movement.

Concern about women's well-being was prominent in the coalition conversation. Other serendipitous timing was that my visit occurred during Ramadan. I observed shelter interactions that highlighted intentional, respectful, caring connections across differences, particularly around fasting and communal meal preparations. These conveyed the sense that the shelter home was a place of cultural and relational learning for all of us passing through.

Relief & Gratitude for Ethnographic Methods

My data collection period was all too brief. Yet I left with relief and gratitude that ethnographic methods had allowed me to embrace how little I knew and identify my misguided preconceptions, and to interact with authenticity, reciprocity, and flexibility, so that I could fully open up to learning through all I experienced. Towards my study goals, I developed a beginning understanding of supportive relationships. The added gift was the personal stretching gained by participating; I did not know I could improvise in the theatrical sense at all, and I gained confidence in improvising as a researcher.

When Ethical Requirements Become a Bane on Qualitative Inquiry in Third World Countries: Reflecting on Studying "Sensitive" Topics as a Ghanaian Student in Canada

Festus Moasun
Wilfrid Laurier University, Waterloo, Canada
moas3180@mylaurier.ca

One of the most difficult, yet undiscussed challenges confronting young researchers who study in institutions in the west and who research in third world countries is the quest to meet the ethical requirements of western institutions. The principal aim of ethics review boards anywhere in the world is to ensure that research participants are protected from harm. Thus, ethical guidelines such as respect for human dignity, respect for free and informed consent, respect for vulnerable persons and respect for the privacy and confidentiality, and balancing harm and benefits of the research among others are prescribed (Tri-Council Policy Statement [TCPS2], 2014).

Typically, while ethics review boards in Western countries appreciate the importance of especially students in their institutions researching topical issues in third world countries, they emphasize protection of participants from harm to the neglect of the benefits of research, not only to the research participants but to the many others who share similar experiences. Hence, the review boards appear to emphasise mitigating harm to research participants without much regards for the need for a balance between harm and benefits as prescribed by TCPS2 of 2014.

Importance of Ethics Reviews

Just so that I am not misunderstood, I am not against ethical scrutiny of research proposals. I am in favour of all researchers subjecting their proposed studies to ethical review in order that the best interests of the research participants are safeguarded. Here, I consider the best interest of research participants to include not only their protection from negative effects of research but also the long term benefits they stand to gain from the outcomes of research, such as policy changes. The Canadian TCP2 suggests that the level of risk of a study must be commensurate with the level of risk of the proposed study. Hence, ethics review boards are enjoined to anticipate potential risks of a study and guide researchers to guard against them.

My concern with ethics review boards of western countries--many of my doctoral colleagues from especially Africa share similar frustrations--is the tendency for a universalisation of risks. Ever heard of the term, sensitive research topics? What is sensitive and who defines it as such are questions that many ethics review boards often tend to ignore. Sensitivity cannot be separated from cultural contexts.

Define sensitivity whichever way, and I will insist that it is more cultural than we think. Taking for example, the feeling of pain, culturally, particularly, in the northern part of Ghana, young men are trained to endure pain for as long as possible. An easy admission of pain on the part of a young man is an exhibition of cowardice. So, for example, in the mornings as we gather around the fire during the harmattan, when a neighbour comes around to pick a few flints of fire to set a mini bonfire for themselves in their homes, we do not need tongs to fetch the flints for them. The nearest young man to the fire picks the flints with his hands without a hint of pain. For the many years that I have experienced this, not many, if any at all, got injured by picking flints of fire with their hands.

Among some tribes in Northern Ghana, some people dance in naked in fire as a form of entertainment. However, to observe a person pick fire with their hands in the West cannot and should not be entertained at all, nor should walking on and through it. Otherwise, such a person might be categorised as self-harming or suicidal. The difference in culture and belief systems in my opinion must require contextual consideration when research proposals are brought before ethics review boards for consideration and approval. However, this does not often appear to be the case.

My "Sensitive" Topic

When I started my PhD, I was poised to study the infanticide of children with disabilities among certain communities in Northern Ghana. This is because while there have been a few studies on the topic such as Allotey and Reidpath (2001), and Denham, Adongo, Freydberg and Hodgson (2010), these studies were both conducted in the same district and even though the authors did not say so, many are under the impression that the act pertains only in communities in this district northern regions of Ghana.

The Killing of My Brother

As a matter of fact, my mother's last-born son--my blood brother--fell victim to this barbaric act of infanticide because he had a developmental disability and was traditionally diagnosed as a spirit child (lipalpaaln) in Likpakpaaln, the language of the Konkomba people of Ghana. My brother is not the only victim of this practice of killing children with disabilities. I had a classmate who lived in an adjourning village to mine who also met same unfortunate faith in the early 1990s. Across the West African Sub-Region, Bayat (2015) reports of similar acts killing children with various forms of differences.

There is no doubt that researching into the topic will help to bring exposure to this undesirable practice and therefore engender discussions as to how to address it at the national level. At the personal level, it will help me bring closure to my continuous grieving for my brother. However, by simply mentioning this topic on a number of occasions to some PhD colleagues, faculty and a prominent member of my school's Ethics Review Board, I was told flatly that I am in for an uphill battle with the latter as the topic was a "sensitive" one and will be met with ethical barriers.

Disarmed and Deprived

At that point, I felt disarmed and deprived of an opportunity to bring closure to my brother's death. I felt disarmed mainly because as an international student with four years of funding, I do not have the luxury of time and financial resources to engage a topic that will take a long time to get ethics approval or never at all. Therefore, I give up for now and console myself with the adage that "he who fights and runs away, lives to fight another time."

Maybe with time, I will learn the tricks of the game and be able to research into such a topic so dear to my heart later in my academic career.

What is worrying to me as a young researcher is that there appears to be a lack of trust on the part of the ethics review boards for qualitative inquirers who engage in what they term as sensitive topics. There is no denying the fact that there are researchers who might abuse research participants in the course of their studies. However, in the case of qualitative inquiry, hardly anyone goes into researching a phenomenon without some form of personal relationship with the phenomenon (Vagle, 2018). To research such topics as infanticide can be unsettling for researchers, especially for those who research in their own communities as they attempt to disrupt long and deep-seated cultural beliefs and practices. Such researchers are most likely to be viewed as traitors to their customs and traditions. Therefore, to be faced with the slightest hint of distrust by the ethics review board is in itself a strong demotivator.

Again, what may be seen as a no-go area in a western research setting in many instances in my experience, could be a very fertile ground for rich qualitative engagement in Ghana and most parts of Africa. For example, while there may be a level of skepticism that one may not be able to access participants to discuss the topic of infanticide in a western society for instance, knowledgeable friends back in my home village have informed me that I can access even the spiritualists who are responsible for the extermination of the "spirit children" for interviews.

If one is ever wondering how this is possible, I wish to draw attention to the fact that this is a matter of culture and belief. As far as the custodians of this culture and beliefs are concerned, they have done nothing wrong to shy away from sharing information on such practices.

It is my conviction that it is time for western ethics review boards to begin to consider ethical concerns, taking into consideration the socio-cultural contexts in which the inquiries take place. They must do so in light of the growing numbers of students who study in western institutions and research in third world countries such as Ghana. After all, the Canadian Tri-Council Policy Statement on ethics in research as amended in 2014, for example, indicates that it does not seek to prescribe definitive answers to ethical questions but rather, provide guiding principles with which to work.

Otherwise, I foresee a number of possibilities in the face of rigid ethical requirements: first, many, especially qualitative inquirers will continue to forego the most important topics and choose those that are easily able to get ethical approvals. Second, some might circumvent ethical processes to achieve their means, which might present more worrying circumstances than those the review boards seek to avoid.

Alternatives

In order that we do not neglect such important but 'sensitive' areas in light of the above challenges, we must adopt creative ways of producing research data in such areas. Hence, a third possibility, one that I think is a more pragmatic way to sourcing data that will be as close as possible to the researcher's own interview data will be to capitalise on technology and follow television news items online, most of which are available publicly via YouTube, for instance, for data on topics of interest.

For example, over the past few months, I have keenly followed YouTube channels of popular television stations in Ghana and have had access to several tens of interviews with persons with disabilities. In the nearest future, my hope is to purposefully transcribe and analyse these interviews which I believe will be rich sources of information for writing articles for publication. I must however caution that such information may come with certain limitations. The researcher in this case is forced to work with what is available and not what is desirable. There are also no possibilities for follow up for clarification.

To facilitate research that is of high interest and importance in non-western countries, I propose that western ethics review boards deepen their understandings of what practices and beliefs mean to the persons within particular cultural contexts and what the consequences are for those practices and beliefs might be. To see practices and meanings from insiders' perspectives appears to be an essential characteristic of effective review boards.

Who defines what is a sensitive topic is central to moving review boards to deepen their understandings of meanings and practices in non-western cultures. My alternative course of action is less than ideal The thought of reviewing publicly available media to study the killing of children with disabilities in Ghana is at best a poor substitute for in-depth qualitative inquiry that I would like to do.

Conclusions

As a student from Ghana, I did not pursue a dissertation topic that had personal meaning to me and that I was highly motivated to do. I did not have the time needed to negotiate the possible ethics concerns the review board was likely to have. Many other students from non-western counties also do not pursue the topics that are their first choices.

Citations

Allotey, P. & Reidpath, D. (2001). Establishing the causes of childhood mortality in Ghana: The "spirit child." *Social Science and Medicine 52*, 1007–12.

Bayat, M. (2015). The stories of 'snake children': Killing and abuse of children with developmental disabilities in West Africa. *Journal of Intellectual Disability Research, 59 (1)*, 1-10. doi: 10.1111/jir.12118

Canadian Institutes of Health Research, Natural Sciences and Engineering Research Council of Canada, and the Social Sciences and Humanities Research Council of Canada (2014). *Tri-Council Policy Statement: Ethical Conduct for Research Involving Humans (TCPS2)*. Available at: http://www.pre.ethics.gc.ca/pdf/eng/tcps2-2014/TCPS_2_FINAL_Web.pdf

Denham, A. R., Adongo, P. B., Freydberg, N. & Hodgson, A. (2010). Chasing spirits: Clarifying the spirit child phenomenon and infanticide in Northern Ghana, *Social Science & Medicine, 71*, 608-615.

Vagle, M. D. (2018). *Crafting Phenomenological research* (2nd Edition). New York: Routledge

Critical Race Theory, Critical Discourse Analysis, & Critical Social Work: Excerpts from an Unpublished Paper

Many articles in this issue of *QISW* refer to critical race theory (CRT). I (Jane Gilgun) thought we could use further information about CRT. With two PhD students (Gilgun, Valandra, & Sharma, 2008). I presented a conference paper on CRT, critical discourse analysis, and critical social work. The following is an excerpt from this unpublished paper. Many of the articles in this issue illustrates the points in this excerpt.

Critical race theory (CRT) is a "discourse of liberation" (Parker & Lynn, 2002, p. 7) whose purpose is to combat racism by bringing often hidden racist practices to light (Decuir & Dixson, 2004; Dunbar, 2008). Critical race theory emerged in the 1970's amidst concerns over the seemingly slowed progress following the gains of the U.S. civil rights era. CRT begins with the premise that in American society, racism is accepted as both normal and natural (Ladson-Billings, 2000). It maintains that progress towards racial social justice is contingent upon the exposure of such racism in all its forms and that such exposure is necessary in the struggle for racial social justice.

Critical race theorists encourage social scientists to examine racist practices from insider perspectives through listening to the stories of persons that racism affects. Critical race theorists seek counter-stories (Chapman, 2007; Solórzano & Yosso, 2002); that is, narratives that encapsulate the experiences, interpretations, and meanings of persons who are members of non-majority racial and ethnic groups. These narratives often are absent from the understandings of members of majority classes, and they cast doubt on the assumptions that members of majority cultures hold.

As Chapman stated, "counter-stories …demonstrate the complexity of people's lived experiences" (p. 160). Critical race theory posits that the study of individual lives can identify culture-wide racist practices and counter-stories, whose exposure are correctives to unequal power relations. Counter-stories are a means of resisting the majority culture's assumptions.

Racism as Permanent

Critical race theory emphasizes permanence of racism in American society and the influence of historical events upon contemporary racist practices (Bell, 1995; DeCuir & Dixson, 2004). While for many members of the majority culture, the legacies of slavery are all but forgotten, for many African-Americans, the history of slavery is part of their identity, if not on a conscious level, as underlying themes related to their self-identity.

Discourses of Resistance

Cool pose is an example of a discourse of resistance, or a counter-story to negative stereotypes of black males in American society. As one of several strategies that African-American males use to cope with "diminished rights and blemished self-esteem" (Majors & Billson, 1992, p. 7) that arises within systems of racism, cool pose encompasses both pro-active, productive behaviors as well as self-defeating behaviors. This discourse identifies itself through outwardly expressive styles of dressing, speaking, and walking that asserts a distinct and often glamorous identity in a world that reflects back few positive images of black males.

In enacting cool pose, black males attempt to create a symbolic universe by engaging in activities that allow the "kaleidoscopic brilliance of the black male self" to shine, since "people are drawn to the power of cool black male because he epitomizes control, strength, and pride" (Majors & Billson, 1992, p. 2). Scholars suggest that some African-American men believe exaggerated physical and sexual prowess is the proper expression of African-American male identity (Akbar, 1996). As Majors and Billson observed, this symbolic universe of cool pose is a "relentless performance" (p. 4) on the part of black males to put forth an impressive image of themselves for the mainstream.

Constructing Symbolic Universes

Cool pose, therefore, helps black men who ascribe to it to construct a "symbolic universe" that provides a haven against the tensions of inhabiting a social space that belittles them. It also carries the potential for "[exacting] a price that seems destructively high" (Majors & Billson, 1992, p. 2) that increases their risks related to violence and low academic and vocational achievement. In addition, when cool pose includes objectifying women and using them sexually, this puts women at risk.

Cool pose can be understood with the context of race relations and race-based violence in the United States. For hundreds of years, the discourse of black males as over-sexed, aggressive, and dangerous has persisted in white American culture, particularly in relation to white women (Bennett, 1966; Collins, 2004; DeGruy-Leary, 2005; Myrdal, 1944; Poulson-Bryant, 2005; Wells-Barnett, 1900; Whitfield, 1991). Many scholars believe that the discourses of slavery continue to scar African-Americans socially and psychologically to this day (Akbar, 1996; Patterson, 1998). Cool pose, then, is both of discourse of positive identity and a discourse of resistance.

Critical Discourse Analysis

Critical discourse analysis (CDA) examines ideologies of power embedded in texts, where texts refer not only to words and language, but also to nonverbal symbols, such as clothing, gestures, body posture, gait, speech inflections, and other tags that accompany the enunciation of words (Gee, 2005; Fairclough, 2001; Wodak, 2001). Texts also include photographs, music, paintings, objects, and landscapes.

The Power of Language

Language as text is more than marks on paper or sounds that flow from mouths to ears. Texts activate images, emotional processes, displays of intention, and behaviors that human beings typically experience as taken-for-granted ways of perceiving and acting in the world. In this perspective, individual action and social structural issues are in mutual interaction, where individuals draw upon culture-wide themes, practices, and beliefs as guidelines or scripts for their own actions, self-representations, and interpretive frameworks, while they simultaneously contribute to these culture-wide themes, beliefs, and practices.

Performing Culture

In brief, individuals enact or perform culture in their own lives, while at the same time they contribute to culture-wide themes, beliefs, and practices (Andersson, 2008; Blommaert & Bulcaen, 2000; Chase, 2005; Kimmel, 2008).

The term *discourse* refers to these cultural practices and beliefs. For some discourse analysts, Discourse or big-D stands for culture-wide beliefs, while discourse or little-d stands for individual enactments (Gee, 2005). Critical discourse analysts also refer to Discourse as grand narratives and discourse as personal narratives. Other analysts use additional terms, such as Wagner and Wodak's (2006) use of the terms "local" for personal, individual actions, which they call performances, and "cultural" patterns and "structural patterns." Still others refer to "interpretive frames" (Alexander, 2006), a term that stands for the discourses that individuals draw from wider culture themes and practices.

Divergent Discourses

Individuals with divergent social statuses and divergent experiences of culture may have difficulty understanding one another because they draw upon divergent discourses or grand narratives to construct their individualized, personal, and local views of proper ways to act in the world. When individuals have power over others because of social location and access to resources, more powerful persons may draw upon their own discourses and misinterpret the discourses of others. Fozdar (2008) refers to the dueling discourses that various "isms" produce, such as sexism and racism and their counter-stories.

Understanding discourses that diverge from one's own requires a grasp of our own discourses and the discourses of others. This means that we understand the points of view of others and our own and have an appreciation of the possibly divergent interpretive frames or discourses that we and others invoke not only through words but through body language, clothing, and other indicators of identity and meanings.

Although some individuals and groups may comply with discourses that more powerful persons put forward, others may resist, contest, and dispute them. For example, the discourses of street gang members could be discourses of resistance. As with other enactments of discourses, individuals who want to be recognized as a member of a particular group, such as street gangs, not only talk in certain ways, but walk in certain ways, behave in certain ways, use symbols such as clothing, gang signs, and graffiti, and are present in particular locales.

Countering Power

These discourses may be counter to the discourses of persons who have social, political, and economic power. Those in power enact their own discourses in their own locales, such as country clubs, waterfront mansions, and expensive cars and have their own symbols in terms of clothing, housing, and ways of talking and otherwise presenting themselves.

CDA is a way of analyzing ideologies of power and resistance to power that is represented in discourse. CRT's counter-stories are similar to discourses of resistance. As Gee (2005) noted, "we use language to get recognized as taking on a certain identity or role, that is, to build an identity here-and-now" (p. 11). More powerful persons may impose identities and other discourses on less powerful individuals (van Dijk, 2006), which may silence the less powerful. The analysis of the constructions and contestation of power and identity are key concerns of CDA. The subjugated and silenced discourses are also the concerns of CDA.

Wagner and Wodak (2006) view individual actions as performances or enactments of more general, cultural patterns. In their analysis of successful career women, they found that the women drew upon multiple discourses and metaphors to represent themselves as successful, including self-made woman and lucky, while they suppressed other discourses related to ambivalence and passivity regarding their success as women.

Methods as Open

CDA does not promote a single approach to analysis, but many. In fact, individuals who want to do a CDA are free to create their own method (Fairclough, 2001; Gee, 2005; Wodak, 2001). van Dijk (2006), for example, advocates for a triangulated approach that looks at 1) social aspects of discourse that includes who has power over whom, 2) the beliefs and ideologies that are embedded in discourse, and 3) the contextual influences on discourses that individuals accept or reject. These contextual influences include contemporaneous as well as historical events.

In summary, the defining characteristics of CRT are race and power, while power associated with language and other symbols defines CDA. In combination, CRT and CDA show promise of being a method for the analysis of race and power as embedded in discourse in general and in social work practice in particular. With their emphasis on social justice and social context, CRT and CDA are a natural fit with social work.

Critical Social Work

Critical race theory and CDA have natural links with critical social work. Each is concerned with power on the social structural and institutional levels. Race, ethnicity, gender, social class, age, and physical and mental ability are among the categories of interest in critical social work. While there are many schools of thought on the components of critical social work, themes that appear within these perspectives include social justice as a value, the idea that social, institutional and structural assumptions and practices affect human lives, the identification of oppressive practices linked to institutions and social structures, and the formulation of actions meant to counteract oppression (Hicks & Pozzuto, 2005).

Critical Reflection

Critical social workers encourage practitioners to reflect upon the links between service users' and their own individual experiences to wider social contexts, including oppressive structures and practices (Yee, 2005) and to combine critical reflection on social processes and grand discourses with action guided by tenets of social justice (Harvey, 1990).

White Privilege

When race is at issue, critical social workers believe that members of the white majority must critically reflect upon and discuss with others whether and how they have experienced privilege and opportunity because of their membership in dominant groups (Yee, 2005). By so doing, white social workers, therefore, may become more open to and more understanding of the discourses and counter-stories that guide service users' lives, assumption, and action. They must continually reflect upon and question their own possibly unexamined discourses that guide their practice.

Citations

Akbar, N. (1996). *Breaking the chains of psychological slavery.* Tallahassee, FL: Mind Productions and Associates.

Alexander, B. K. (2006). *Performing black masculinity: Race, culture, and queer identity.* Lanham, MD: Altamira.

Andersson, K. (2008). Constructing young masculinity: A case study of heroic discourse on violence. *Discourse & Society, 19(2)*, 139-161.

Bell, D.A. (1995). *Faces at the bottom of the well: The permanence of racism.* New York: Basic.

Bennett, L.J. (1966). Before the Mayflower: A history of the Negro in America. Chicago: Johnson.

Blommaert, J. & Bulcaen, C. (2000). Critical discourse analysis. *Annual Review of Anthropology, 29(1)*, 447-466.

Chase, S. E. (2005). Narrative inquiry: Multiple lenses, approaches, voices. In N. K. Denzin & Y. S. Lincoln (Eds.), *The Sage handbook of qualitative research* (3rd ed.) (pp. 651-679). Thousand Oaks, CA: Sage.

Collins, P.H. (2004). *Black sexual politics: African Americans, gender, and the new racism.* New York: Routledge.

DeGruy-Leary, J. (2005). *Post-traumatic slave syndrome: America's legacy of enduring injury and healing.* Milwa, OR: Uptone Press.

Decuir, J. T., & Dixson, A.D. (2004) "So when it comes out, they aren't that surprised that it is there:" Using critical race theory as a tool of analysis of race and racism in education. *Educational Researcher 33(5)*, 26-31.

Dunbar, C. Jr. (2008). Critical race theory and indigenous methodologies. In N.K. Denzin & Y.S. Lincoln (Eds.). *Critical race theories and indigenous methodologies* (pp. 85-100). Thousand Oaks, CA: Sage.

Fairclough, N. (2001). *Language and power* (2nd ed.). Essex, UK: Pearson.

Fozdar, F. (2008). Dueling discourses, shared weapons: Rhetorical techniques used to challenge racist arguments. *Discourse & Society, 19(4)*, 529-541.

Gee, J. P. (2005). *An introduction to discourse analysis: Theory and method* (2nd. ed.). New York: Routledge.

Gilgun, Jane F, Valandra, Alankaar Sharma (2008, April 18). Critical race theory and critical discourse analysis as tools to examine race and racism in social work practice and research. Paper presented at the

Midwest Qualitative Research Conference, St. Thomas University, St. Paul, Minnesota, USA, April 18.

Hicks, S., & Pozzuto, R. (2005). Introduction: Towards "becoming" a critical social worker. In S. Hicks, J. Fook, & R. Pozzuto (Eds.), *Social work: A critical turn* (pp. ix-xviii). Toronto: Thompson.

Harvey, L. (1990). *Critical social research.* London: Unwin Hyman.

Kimmel, M. S. (2008). Th*e gendered society* (3rd ed.) New York: Oxford University.

Ladson-Billings, G. (2000). Racialized discourses and ethnic epistemologies. In N. K. Denzin & Y. S. Lincoln (Eds). *Handbook of qualitative research* (2nd ed.) (pp. 257-276). Thousand Oaks, CA: Sage.

Ladson-Billings, G. & Donnor, J. (2005). The moral activist role of critical race scholarship. In N. K. Denzin & Y. S. Lincoln (Eds.) *Handbook of qualitative research* (3rd ed.) (pp. 279-277). Thousand Oaks, CA: Sage.

Lee-See, L.A. (1998). Human behavior theory and the African American experience. *Journal of Human Behavior in the Social Environment, 1(2/3),* 7- 29.

Lillian, D. L. (2007). A thorn by any other name: Sexist discourse as hate speech. *Discourse & Society, 18(6),* 719-740.

Majors, R. & Billson, J.M. (1992). *Cool pose: The dilemmas of black manhood in America.* New York: Simon & Schuster.

Manning M.C., Cornelius, L.J., & Okundaye, J.N. (2004). Empowering African Americans through social work practice: Integrating an Afrocentric perspective, ego psychology, and spirituality. *Families in Society, 85(2),* 225-231

Mellon, J. (2002). *Bullwhip days: The slave remember: An oral history.* New York: Grove/Atlantic.

Parker, L., & Lynn, M. (2002). What's race got to do with it? Critical race theory's conflict with and connection to qualitative research methodology and epistemology. *Qualitative Inquiry, 8(1),* 7-22.

Poulson-Bryant, S. (2005). *Hung: A meditation on the measure of black men in America.* New York: Doubleday.

Solórzano, D. G., & Yosso, T. J. (2002). Critical race methodology: Counter-story as an analytic framework in education research. *Qualitative Inquiry, 8(1),* 23-44.

Sue, D. W. et al (2007). Racial microaggression in everyday life: Implications for clinical practice. *American Psychologist, 62(4),* 271-286.

Van Dijk, T. (2001). Principles of critical discourse analysis. In Wetherell, M., Taylor, S., & Yates, S. J. (Eds.), *Discourse theory and practice: A reader,* pp. 300-317, London, UK: Sage.

Wagner, I. & R. Wodak (2006). Performing success: Identifying strategies of self-preservation in women's biographical narratives. *Discourse & Society, 17(3),* 385-411.

Wells-Barnett, I.B. (1900). Lynch law in America. *The Arena, 23 (1)*, 15-24.

Whitfield, S.J. (1991). *A death in the delta: The story of Emmett Till.* Baltimore: John Hopkins University Press

Wodak, Ruth (2001). What CDA is about. In Ruth Wodak & Michael Myers (Eds.), *Methods of critical discourse analysis* (pp. 1-13). London: Sage.

Yee, J. Y. (2005). Critical anti-racism praxis: The concept of whiteness implicated. In S. Hicks, J. Fook, & R. Pozzuto (Eds.), *Social work: A critical turn* (pp. 87-103). Toronto: Thompson.

User Involvement in Sami Perspectives and Context: Indigenous Mental Health Care in Norway

Rita Sørly
Norut Northern Research Institute, Norway
rita.sorly@uit.no

To me, as with many Norwegians today, my ethnic origin is unknown. My grandfather's ancestors came from the Swedish side of Tornedalen, the Torne valley. Tornedalen is an area well known for being an area of Lapland. The colonization of the Sami people through the ages has, however, led to our ethnic identity being complex and in a state of transitions. I have children that identify themselves as Sami. They have been adopted as grandchildren by my best friend, a 75 year-old Sami woman.

A Sami Language Children's Book

My youngest son, Ørn (his name is "Eagle" in English), has, since he was a little boy, been able to communicate with his akkhu (grandmother in Sami language) in Sami. Recently we published a children book together, both in Northern Sami gielli (Northern Sami language) and Norwegian; "Namako and the tentacles -Namkao ja bivdojuolggit." My son wants children to be able to learn both languages.

The book is about two researchers looking for the giant octopus in the deep sea. My son's akkhu, Rauni Magga Lukkari, is a famous Sami author and poet, and she has translated the text from Norwegian to Northern Sami. She had to find ten new Sami words and our project is recognized as a language development project.

Indigenous Mental Health Research

My belonging to the ethnically diverse landscape of northern Norway has led to a great interest in indigenous mental health research. I am currently leading a research project, in collaboration with Sami National Competence Center on Mental Health and Substance Abuse, on user involvement in mental health care in Sami perspectives and context. The Sami are an indigenous people living in Norway, Sweden, Finland, and Russia. The Sami population of Norway is estimated to be 40,000(Statistics Norway 2010).

History

Historically, the Sami were reindeer herders, small-scale farmers, and fishermen (Blix et al., 2012). National states have made strong efforts to assimilate the Sami people into the majority populations, and the Sami have experienced stigmatization and discrimination (Blix, 2013). The assimilation process in Norway is called the period of "Norwegianization" (Niemi, 1997), and reflects a dark period in the country.

During the 1960's and 1970s, in a time of general increase of living standards and improvements in the welfare and health care systems in Norway, and ethnic revitalization process started. Gradually the Sami political power movement established itself on the Nordic stage, but it is still a complicated, diverse landscape characterized by cultural diversity.

Challenges to Mental Health Care

This poses challenges to mental health care in many ways. Culture influences the experience, expression, course and outcome of mental health distress, help-seeking and the response to health promotion and treatment interventions (Kirmayer, 2012). Standardized mental health services tailored to the needs of the majority population focus on diagnoses and disabilities, and overshadows an approach that understands, appreciates and emphasizes Sami thinking, values, history and everyday life.

User Involvement

There is little research-based knowledge about how user involvement can be understood and implemented in a Sami mental health context. The dominant, Norwegian culture, is expressed through social institutions, including the health care system, and regulates what sorts of problems and what kind of social or cultural differences that are worth attention (ibid.).

In this project. we are interviewing Sami mental health care users and health professionals working in Sami core areas. The main objective is to investigate how increased user involvement for Sami mental health care users can be understood and exercised in the meeting with healthcare practitioners.

Goal: User-Friendly Services

We want to investigate whether a local understanding of user involvement can provide new insights in relation to more user-friendly services. We have two Sami co-researchers with us in the project, both with own experiences from the services. They will help us, investigating whether the Sami people suffer from health disparities and social disadvantage as a result of the meanings of their socially constructed identities. We will keep you updated.

Citations

Blix, Bodil Hansen, Hamran, Torunn, & Normann, Hans Ketil (2012). Indigenous life stories as narratives of health and resistance: A dialogical narrative analysis. *Canadian Journal of Nursing Research, 44(2)*, 64-85.

Blix, Bodil Hansen, Hamran, Torunn, & Normann, Hans Ketil (2013). Struggles of being and becoming: A dialogical narrative analysis of the life stories of Sami elderly. *Journal of Aging Studies, 27(3)*, 264-275.

Kirmayer, Laurence J. (2012). Rethinking cultural competence. Transcultural psychiatry 49(2), 149-164.

Niemi, Einar (1997). Sami history and the frontier myth: A perspective on northern Sami spatial and rights history. *Sami Culture in a New Era: The Norwegian Sami Experience.* Kárásjohka/Karasjok: Davvi Girji, 62-85.

Gaski, Harald (Ed.) (1997) *Sami culture in a new era. The Norwegian Sami experience,* Kárásjohka/Karasjok: Davvi Girji, 62-85.

Statistics Norway. (2010). *Samisk statistikk 2010* (Sami statistics 2010). Oslo: Kongsvinger, Statistisk sentralbyrå.

Sørly, Rita (2018). *Namako og tentaklene--Namako ja bivdojuolggit.* Gollegiella

<u>*New Edition*</u>
An Excerpt on Grounded Theory & Deductive Qualitative Analysis from the Second Edition of the *Sage Handbook on Grounded Theory*

Jane Gilgun
University of Minnesota, Twin Cities, USA
jgilgun@umn.edu

Tony Bryant and Kathy Charmaz have edited a second edition of *The Sage Handbook of Grounded Theory* that will be published in 2019. I'm pleased

that I have a chapter in this edition. The chapter is called Deductive Qualitative Analysis and Grounded Theory: Sensitizing Concepts and Hypothesis-Testing.

Here is an excerpt, with some minor additions.

Deductive qualitative analysis (DQA) is one of three approaches to research associated with the Chicago School of Sociology. The other two are grounded theory and field research, which is descriptive in nature, and sometimes referred to as ethnographic research. DQA is an updating of analytic induction (AI), which is an approach older than GT and that is also associated with the Chicago School.

Theory and Qualitative Inquiry
Deductive qualitative analysis and its predecessor AI allow for qualitative hypothesis testing theory testing as well as concept-guided descriptive research, which is research that begins with sensitizing concepts. The use of sensitizing concepts is traditional in the Chicago School for decades before Blumer (1969) gave them a name (Gilgun, 1999, 2005, 2016). Each of these three types produce findings that are grounded in data on which findings are based.

The defining characteristics of DQA are 1) the use of concepts and/or hypotheses from the onset of the research, 2) positive case analysis that involves the search for data whose meanings might lead to modifications, refutations, and reformulations of concepts and hypotheses, both the initial material and the material that researchers develop over the course of research, and 3) embeddedness in the perspectives of the Chicago School of Sociology.

The Chicago School of Social Work Research

The Chicago School goes back to the early part of the twentieth century (Bulmer, 1984; Deegan, 1990; Faris, 1967; Fine, 1995; Forte, 2004; Gilgun, 1999; Low & Bowden, 2013). While there is more than one Chicago School, I am focusing on research methods, methodologies, and philosophies developed in the first part of the twentieth century and whose legacies extend to this day....

Social workers such as Jane Addams, Sophinisba Breckinridge, and Edith Abbott made substantial contributions to the Chicago School of Sociology, not only in terms of research methods and methodologies such as ethics of care, immersion, first-hand experience, social change, importance of context, multiple points of view, reflexivity, but also in terms of formulating American pragmatism and symbolic interactionism that are the philosophical bases of Chicago School inquiry (Bulmer, 1994; Deegan, 1990; Forte, 2004; Gilgun, 1999, 2012, 2014, 2015, 2016, in press; Hamington, 2018). I think I can make a case for a Chicago School of Social Work Research.

A Way of Thinking

The idea that DQA is a way of thinking is important to the case I make in this chapter. In making the case, I am following in the footsteps of researchers associated with the Chicago School of Sociology. Bob Bogdan (Bogdan & Biklen, 2007), who through his teaching and writing has guided many researchers in how they do fieldwork, or descriptive qualitative research, pointed out that qualitative research is about thinking conceptually.

Bodgan said about his training in fieldwork, also sometimes called ethnography, with Blanche Geer (Becker, Geer, & Hughes, 1968; Becker, Geer, Hughes, & Strauss, 1961): "Blanche modeled how to think conceptually. What I got out of her seminar was not the content. She was teaching a way of thinking" (Gilgun, 1992, p. 9).

Geer earned a Ph.D. in sociology from the University of Chicago and is a researcher in the tradition of the Chicago School of Sociology. Glaser (1978) emphasized the centrality of ideas in qualitative research and for sociology in general: "Good ideas contribute the most to the science of sociology" (p. 8).

Also, Strauss (1992) wrote, grounded theory "is a general way of thinking about analysis" (p. 2). The power of qualitative methods resides in the thinking that guide the research, the ideas behind the methods help develop, and the trustworthiness and authenticity of findings.

Initial Concepts & Hypotheses

In DQA, researchers begin their studies with concepts and hypotheses with the hope that the conceptual material will aid their thinking in terms of the insights they provide and the directions of inquiry they suggest. In brief, concepts and hypotheses in DQA serve sensitizing purposes in the spirit of Blumer's (1969) ideas about sensitizing concepts.

Researchers using DQA are curious and not doctrinaire about the helpfulness of initial conceptual material. I, for example, begin my research with the hope that the initial material will help me see what I might otherwise not have seen and that the analysis in which I engage will led to refutation and reformulation of the initial material and thus to a closer fit between the resulting conceptual material and the data that are the foundation of my theorizing.

Hypothesis Testing

One of the clearest examples of research that begins with hypotheses and that involves the modification of hypotheses during data collection and analysis is the study of Cressey (1950, 1953) of embezzlers.

Cressey began with a hypothesis that he developed from research by Sutherland (1937, 1949) on white collar crime that posited that embezzlers consider embezzlement a technical violation and ended with the hypothesis that embezzlers. His final hypothesis was embezzlers consider embezzlement to be illegal and to be a violation of financial trust that arises from seeking solutions to non-shareable problems.

Scientific Method

At their core, the procedures of DQA compose a form of scientific method, with scientific method involving hypotheses, tests of hypotheses, and revisions (Anderson & Hepburn, 2015: Osbeck, 2014; Yuan, 2005), or conjectures, refutations, and reformulations (Popper, 1959). In DQA, the initial conceptual material composes the conjectures, and positive case analysis and related procedures of analysis are the vehicles for refutations. Researchers refute and reformulate part or all of the conceptual material when their interpretations of data provide the evidence to do so.

Blumer (1969), who used the term sensitizing concepts to describe initial material, described them as notions that help researchers to focus their inquiries and to notice and name aspects of phenomena they might otherwise have overlooked.

Sensitizing Concepts

Blumer's understanding of sensitizing concepts is a principle upon which I base DQA. Along with Waller (1934) and others from the Chicago School, Blumer also pointed out that, as helpful as initial concepts and theory are, they also may blind researchers to other aspects of phenomena that might be significant to their understandings. Such a consequence of the use of initial theory led researchers to purposefully think about and search for exceptions to their emerging findings. They gave the search for exceptions the name negative case analysis (Becker, 1953; Cressey, 1950, 1953; Gilgun, 1995, 2001, 2007, 2014; 2015; Znaniecki, 1934). Researchers sought negative cases in order to revise emerging findings so that their thinking accounts for exceptions and contradictions and thus ensures more fully for possible diversity in findings.

Search for Exceptions

In DQA, the term positive case analysis takes the place of the term negative case analysis because the search for exceptions and the desire for diversity of findings are positive goals. Positive case analysis guides researchers to construct theory and descriptions that account for patterns and exceptions to general patterns over the course of the research. Consistent with notions of indeterminacy (Charmaz, 2014), the findings of DQA are provisional, subject to revision when researchers have evidence to do so.

Findings as Provisional

Recognition of the provisional nature of research findings has a long history in the Chicago School. For instance, Thomas & Znaniecki (1927), early contributors to the Chicago School, stated that, although they sought to develop "generally applicable conclusions," they did not consider their work on Polish immigrants in Europe and the United States as giving "any definitive and universally valid sociological truths' (pp, 340-341).

Rather, they said that their work is suggestive and prepares the ground for further research. Cressey (1950), at the end of his account of the multiple times that he changed his theory of embezzlement during data collection and analysis, wrote about his final hypothesis: "the fact that it was revised several times probably means that future revisions will be necessary" (p. 743).

Citations

Anderson, Hanne & Hepburn, Brian (2015). Scientific method. *Stanford Encyclopedia of Philosophy.* http://plato.stanford.edu/entries/scientific-method/

Becker, Howard S. (1953). Becoming a marihuana user. *American Journal of Sociology, 59,* 235-242.

Becker, Howard S., Blanche Geer, Everett C. Hughes, & Anselm L. Strauss, A. L. (1961). *Boys in white: Student culture in medical school.* Chicago: University of Chicago Press.

Becker, Howard S., Geer, B., & Hughes, E. (1968). *Making the grade.* New York: Wiley.

Blumer, Herbert (1969). What is wrong with social theory? In Herbert Blumer (1969/1986), *Symbolic interactionism.* (pp. 140-152) Berkeley: University of California Press.

Bogdan, Robert C., & Sarri Sari K. (1992). *Qualitative research for education* (2nd ed.). Boston: Allyn & Bacon.

Bulmer, Martin (1984). *The Chicago School of Sociology: Institutionalization, diversity, and the rise of sociological research.* Chicago: University of Chicago Press.

Charmaz, Kathy (2014). *Constructing grounded theory: A practical guide through qualitative analysis* (2nd ed.). London: Sage. Kindle edition.

Cressey, Donald R. (1950). Criminal violation of financial trust. *American Sociological Review, 15 (6),* 738-743.

Cressey, Donald R. (1953). *Other people's money.* Glencoe, IL: Free Press.

Deegan, Mary Jo. (1990). *Jane Addams and the men of the Chicago School,* 1892-1918. New Brunswick, N. J.: Transaction.

Forte, James A. (2004). Symbolic interactionism and social work: A forgotten legacy. Part 1. *Families in Society, 85(3),* 391-400.

Gilgun, Jane F. (1992). Field methods training in the Chicago School traditions: The early career of Bob Bogdan. *Qualitative Family Research, 6(1),* 8-11.

Gilgun, Jane F. (1999). Methodological pluralism and qualitative family research. In Suzanne K. Steinmetz, Marvin B. Sussman, and Gary W. Peterson (Eds.), *Handbook of Marriage and the Family* (2nd ed.) (pp. 219-261). New York: Plenum

Gilgun Jane F. (2001, November). "Case Study Research, Analytic Induction, and Theory Development: The Future and the Past," (2001, November) paper presented at the 31st Preconference Workshop on Theory Development and Research Methodology, National Conference on Family Relations, Rochester, NY, November. Basis of an article published in Journal of Family Psychology, 2005.

Gilgun, Jane F. (2005). Qualitative research and family psychology. *Journal of Family Psychology, 19(1),* 40-50.

Gilgun Jane F. (2007, November). "The Legacy of the Chicago School of Sociology for Family Theory-Building," (2 Paper presented at the pre-Conference Workshop on Theory Construction and Research Methodology, National Council on Family Relation, Pittsburgh, PA, November 9.

Gilgun, Jane F. (2012). Enduring themes in qualitative family research. *Journal of Family Theory and Review, 4*, 80-95.

Gilgun, Jane F. (2014). Writing up qualitative research. In Patricia Leavy (Ed.). *The Oxford handbook of qualitative research methods* (pp. 658-676). New York: Oxford University

Gilgun, Jane F. (2015). Research and theory building in social work. In William Nichols (Ed.), *Encyclopedia of Social and Behavioral Sciences* (2nd ed.) (pp. 502-507. New York: Elselvier.

Gilgun, Jane F. (2016, November). Deductive qualitative analysis and the search for black swans. Paper presented at the Theory Construction and Research Methodology Preconference Workshop on Theory Construction and Research Methodology held in Minneapolis, MN, USA, November 1.

Gilgun, Jane F. (in press). Deductive qualitative analysis and grounded theory: Sensitizing concepts and hypothesis testing. To appear in Bryant, A. & Charmaz, K. (Eds.), *The Sage handbook of grounded theory* (2nd ed. (. Thousand Oaks, CA: Sage.

Hamington, Maurice (2018). Jane Addams. Stanford Encyclopedia of Philosophy. https://plato.stanford.edu/entries/addams-jane/

Osbeck, Lisa (2014) Scientific reasoning as sense-making: Implications for qualitative inquiry. *Qualitative Psychology 1(1)*, 34-46.

Popper Karl R. (1959). The logic of scientific discovery. New York: Basic.

Strauss, Anselm (1992). A personal history of grounded theory. *Qualitative Family Research, 5(2)*, 1-2.

Thomas, William I., & Znaniecki, Florian (1918-1920). *The Polish peasant in Europe and America*, Vol. 1-2. New York: Knopf.

Waller, Willard (1934). Insight and the scientific method. *American Journal of Sociology, XL*, 285-297.

Yuan, Y.H. (2005). *On the scientific method learned from Albert Einstein in 2005—the World Year of Physics*. Ithaca, NY: Cornell University Library. https://arxiv.org/abs/physics/0510124

Znaniecki, Florian (1934). *The method of sociology*. New York: Farrar & Rinehart.

Rita Sørly Selected to be Editor of a Journal: A New, Old Relationship

Rita Sørly
Norut Northern Research Institute, Norway
rita.sorly@uit.no

I was at the amazing aquarium in Cape Town, South Africa, when I got the phone call. I was admiring manta rays, turtles, tropical fish, the Japa-

nese kobudai, the sheepshead wrasse that changes sexes, a hermaphroditic species that have both female and male organs. I thought of the story I once heard of the Japanese diver Hiroyuki Arakawa who has had a 30-year relationship with a sheepshead wrasse in Japan's Tateyama Bay, where he is the caretaker for an underwater Shinto shrine. He calls the fish, named "Yoriko," by hitting a bell on the underwater shrine.

Hieroyuki saved Yoriko when the fish was severely injured and could not catch food herself. He gave her five crabs every day for ten days until she recovered. He thinks Yoriko remember his actions and wants to show her gratitude.

Relationships

Relationships can take many different forms and shapes. The phone call was from a well-known Norwegian publishing house. The woman on the phone wanted me to become the new editor of one of their journals. I held my breath. I had to keep the same calm as the turtle in the big pool in front of me. I hoped she was talking about The Journal of Mental Health Care. I have had a long relationship with the journal. We have been, to me, close friends since the birth of the journal in 2004.

The field of local-based municipal mental health work is a quite new field of knowledge in Norway and the Nordic countries. With its short academic history, it is still in need of systematic knowledge development. I was so happy to get the call, I started laughing into the phone. I told the woman that I was in South-Africa and that I came here to meet my husband after he had been gone for two months working in Antarctica.

Would You Like to be Editor?

I told her that I almost hadn't slept while I was waiting to see him at the breakfast table every morning. I said that seeing him now, standing beside octopus and jellyfish, while she asked me whether I would like to become editor of my favorite academic journal, was almost too much. I asked her if she liked aquariums as much as I do. She said "I think you're the right person for this mission". I hope so. I am humble and filled with expectations of the great task I will address from January 1, 2019.

The Journal for Mental Health Care is aimed at disseminating knowledge and communicates theory, research, professional development, clinical experience, and debate in mental health work. The journal is the only journal in its field in the Nordic countries.

The journal's contributors include mental health users, professionals, clinicians, government officials, teachers and researchers from different traditions and with different perspectives on mental health.

The journal's purpose is to be representative of different traditions and perspectives on mental health and contribute to debate within the field of study. Articles can be published in Norwegian, Swedish and Danish. We also accept scientific articles in English.

The Journal for Mental Health Care is aimed at students and staff in higher education in mental health, politicians and health authorities, health professionals in health care and professionals and mental health users who work together on mental health.
Link to the journal: https://www.idunn.no/tph

Research Findings into a Scripted Play for Community Building on School Discipline

Priscilla Gibson
University of Minnesota, Twin Cities, USA
pgibson@umn.edu

If you have ever had your research findings presented beyond the typical academic arenas, you surely will resonate with my feelings of total joy  and thoughts of a dream come true when findings from one of my studies was translated into a play performed for community audiences.

In my case, the dialogue was about race, school suspensions, and relationships between families and school staff. It started quite ordinarily with a simple request to present my research on African American grandmother caregivers' experiences with out-of-school suspensions. After the presentation, another researcher (Dr. Sonia Brady) and I were approached by Dr. Catherine Squires, one of the organizers, about joining an interdisciplinary team to bring our respective findings to the public due to concerns about the disproportionate suspension rates of African American students in public schools.

We obtained funding to hire a teaching artist (David Melendez) and student performers. Dr. Brady and I acted as consultants to the process, enthusiastically reading the script and revisions and attending rehearsals.

The play was performed at various venues including at the School of Social Work. Audience members, a mixture of professionals, parents and students, viewed the performances as a preview to discussing questions about institutional problems and stressors that they encounter in schools. Members were placed in a small group with facilitators after the performance to connect the script to their own educational experiences and challenges. They eagerly provided their personal stories and offered suggestions for alternative behaviors, school practices and social policies.

Another Performance of Interviews

The Red Doors Will Never Close: A Performance of an Oral History

Jane Gilgun
University of Minnesota, Twin Cities, USA
jgilgun@umn.edu

The Red Doors Will Never Close is a performance of an oral history project I am conducting at St. John's Episcopal Church in Minneapolis, MN, USA. I wrote the script based on oral history interviews I conducted starting in 2013. Oral histories are people's histories, and they lend themselves to performance. The performers sat in a semi-circle and told stories of events that took place in the 1970s and early 1980s when the church lost more than half of its members.

Those who remained become a close-knit group determined to carry on. They prevailed, and St. John's is one of the most progressive and healthy parishes in Minnesota. All but three of the narrators were in their 80s, and their stories provoked much admiration, pride, and laughter. The emcee was a stage actor who also helped direct the performance.

The Historical Context

People left over issues related to changes in Sunday services and the welcoming of lesbian and gay persons into the congregation, many of whom took leadership positions in advocating for lesbian and gay rights and in demonstrating against the war in Viet Nam and the uses of nuclear power. During that time, the Episcopal church had moved from a penitential to an emphasis on dignity, inclusion, and social justice. Many members of St. John's embraced this new theology and the resulting activism, while others did not. They moved to more conservative churches or left religion all together.

My Experience

This was a wonderful experience for me. I spent time with people whose values I share and who had the courage to carry on in the face of great loss. They created a church that attracts people who want a spiritual community based on shared values and attracts parents . who want to raise their children in a loving, inclusive community. I am a member of St. John's, but I could not be there if the people who told these stories had not created a community whose values I share. Through the oral history project, I am promoting an institution that embodies these values.

I also had an opportunity to experiment with writing plays. I have written one other on the legend of Hannah Robinson, an 18th century woman who defied her wealthy father to marry the man she loved. https://www.amazon.co.uk/Hannah-Robinson-Celebrated-Beauty-Her-ebook/dp/B003E4898O   I have a background in English lit, and I enjoy various types of writing.

Dissemination

The script of The Red Doors is available at https://www.amazon.de/Red-Doors-Will-Never-Close-ebook/dp/B073WWVMKT.   I made a video that is available at https://www.youtube.com/watch?v=Eq6TLEBRqT4.

You can see that I am disseminating the findings of this project in several ways. I've done a conference paper with Laura Moulton, who was then a graduate student, and we are about to submit a paper based on that presentation to an academic journal.

I remember being enthralled decades ago when Helen Kivnick joined the faculty at the University of Minnesota, Twin Cities, USA, School of Social Work, and wrote and sang songs based on her qualitative interviews with elders.

I hope we as social workers continue to find innovate ways of sharing our research. To confine dissemination to academic audiences cuts out practitioners, legislators, program planners, parents, and the public in general. We will enhance the common good if we join the conversations that are part of public discourse and that influence public policy.

Being a social worker means being an advocate. A great way to advocate is through innovative ways of disseminating our work.

PUBLICATIONS CONNECTED TO SOCIAL WORK DAY

If We Create Welcoming Spaces, Who Knows What Will Result?

For a wonderful read, I recommend My Mother's Skull is Burning: A Story of Stories, published on-line in July's Qualitative Inquiry. Authors are Rita Sørly, Bengt Karlsson, & Alec Grant. This is a performance ethnography where three qualitative social work mental health researchers talk to each other on topics that cover a lot of ground that is important to them. Here is the abstract.

> Performing autoethnography is a dynamic and dialogic exercise, transgressing and exceeding traditional expectations of academic papers. In this freely spoken piece—of narratives, thoughts, poems, and reflections—you will meet three international mental health scholar-researchers seeking and deepening connection through friendship. The article began as a single story and developed, as stories often do, to become many stories. It is conversational, shifting discursively across many topics, including diagnosis, medication, mental health demedicalization and recovery, cultural colonization, language, narrative and human abuse, identity, human connection, being outside the academic mainstream, ethnicity, time, and transitions. It is a story of telling stories.

The three authors attributed the origins of the article to an invitation I extended for Rita to do a TED-like talk at Social Work Day 2017. The article shows that when scholars have spaces like Social Work Day in which to share their experiences and their reflections on experiences, many other wonderful things can happen as a result. In this case, a journal article that is a wonderful example of qualitative inquiry. The article is on-line at http://journals.sagepub.com.ezp2.lib.umn.edu/doi/pdf/10.1177/1077800418787547

Rita is an editor for the Nordic regions for *QISW* and wrote an article on research with the Sami of Norway for this first issue of *QISW*.

Jane Gilgun
jgilgun@umn.edu

<u>***Call for Papers***</u>

A Special Collection of Papers Presented at Social Work Day

The editors of *Qualitative Social Work: Research and Practice* invite presenters at Social Work Day to submit papers for a special collection. This is our chance to show the fine work we are presenting at Social Work Day.

Submission

Deadline for submissions is 7 January 2019. Please submit your completed manuscripts to Manuscript Central at *Qualitative Social Work*. The guidelines are located at https://us.sagepub.com/en-us/nam/journal/qualitative-social-work#submission-guidelines. The link to Manuscript Central is also there.

In your cover letter, please state that your submission is for the special issue for Social Work Day. On the cover page of the manuscript, please state the year in which you presented the paper at Social Work Day.

Be Familiar with *Qualitative Social Work*

We suggest that you study articles from *Qualitative Social Work* and identify one or more whose style fits with how you are planning to structure your article. Use these papers as additional guidelines for writing yours. You may write to Jane Gilgun, editor of the special issue, jgilgun@umn.edu, for any questions you have.

Eligibility

Any paper that is unpublished and that was presented at Social Work Day between 2011 and 2018 is eligible. Manuscripts are from 4,000 to 7,000 words in length.

What We Are Looking For

We are interested in publishing a collection of papers from Social Work Day that show the range of types of inquiry that qualitative social work researchers do. Please review articles in this first issue of *Qualitative Inquiry in Social Work* and those published in *Qualitative Social Work* to get an idea of the range.

Decisions & Revisions

Initial decisions will be made by the special issue editors within six weeks of receiving the manuscripts. The decisions are accept, accept with minor revisions, revise and re-submit, and reject.

Contingency Plan

If we have the good fortune to have more papers than is possible to publish in this special collection, we will suggest journals that we think would be interested in the papers we do not choose.

Need for Reviewers

If you would like to become a reviewer for this special collection, please send your name, your affiliation, and your publishing experience to Jane Gilgun, jgilgun@umn.edu. If you are planning to submit a paper for the special issue, we have procedures to maintain impartiality.

AN ANNOUNCEMENT

Ask Dr. Debra (& Colleagues)

Have questions? Wondering? Don't know? The desire for mentoring has been a theme at Social Work Day from the beginning. PhD students, new professors, and more seasoned professors often want to connect with others who are willing to share their experiences. A regular feature of *Qualitative Inquiry in Social Work* will be the Ask Dr. Debra column, modeled after advice columns that appear in newspapers and on-line.

Debra Nelson-Gardell, developmental editor of *QISW* and a beloved mentor, will receive the queries. She and other editors will respond. We will all learn from the questions and the responses.

When I was a new professor, I couldn't figure out how to write a journal article in 20 to 25 pages. I'm better at it now, but it's still a challenge for some types of articles such as a piece on factors associated with good outcomes when children complex trauma. This is just one example of the many questions researchers and inquirers might have. There are many other real-life issues that even senior qualitative inquirers experience.

All questions about qualitative inquiry are welcome. Send your questions to Debra at dnelsong@sw.ua.edu.

Fifteenth International Congress of Qualitative Inquiry

May 15-18, 2019

Theme: Qualitative Inquiry and the Politics of Resistance

Got any ideas for a presentation at Social Work Day 2019? The Congress is now accepting abstracts. The deadline is 1 December 2018. The theme of the 2019 Congress and Social Work Day is Qualitative Inquiry and the Politics of Resistance. To relay the abstract to Social Work Day, check the box on the submission form for social work. The link to the submissions process is https://icqi.org/home/submission/ For an overview of the 2019 year's Congress, click on this link. https://icqi.org Social Work Day is on Thursday, 16 May 2019. Inexpensive housing is at Presby Hall. Here is the link. http://icqi.org/travel/hotel/

For Social Work Day, we'd like to see papers that show what resistance looks like in qualitative social work. We social workers know about resistance because this is what we do. We base our resistance on our vision for a just and caring world.

We would like presentations on any social work-related topic, and we are especially interested in critical race theory, other critical theories, indigenous research, theatre of the oppressed and other arts-based inquiries, critical grounded theory and deductive qualitative analysis, the phenomenology of resistance, community-based action research, teaching qualitative research, reflexivity, writing for publication, and anything that shows how social work inquiry contributes to a more just and caring world. In fact, any approach that centers the experiences of research participants is part of a politics of resistance.

If you would like to join the Social Work Day organizing committee, email Jane Gilgun at jgilgun@umn.edu and share how you would like to contribute to SWD.

See you in Urbana for the great qualitative social work get-together. We are a global enterprise.

A History of Social Work Day

By Jane Gilgun
University of Minnesota, Twin Cities, USA
jgilgun@umn.edu

Social Work Day began in 2011 at the Seventh Annual International Congress of Qualitative Inquiry (ICQI), although inklings of what was to come were present from the first Congress held in 2005. At the first six Congresses, Karen Staller and I organized impromptu meetings of social workers, including lunches and dinners. The desire to be together, learn from each other, and to draw energy and encouragement from each other was present from the first Congress.

Karen remembers, "posting hand written flyers, corralling social workers in the hallways, meeting with groups of new-found friends (already international in constituency) in the cavernous food court after the vendors had closed for the day, and noisy Chinese dinners around huge tables just off campus."

At the second Congress, Karen Staller and I presented a session on evidence-based practice (EBP) in social work that went well[KM5]. Norman Denzin, the founding director of ICQI, invited Karen and me to be presenters on EBP for the pre-conference workshops the following year. Norman has a long-term interest in EBP and the politics of evidence.

This was one of the first indicators that Norman was a promoter of qualitative inquiry in social work. I think he[KM6] wants to promote qualitative social work because of social work's values of justice, care, dignity, worth, autonomy, and competence as well as ecological perspectives, starting where clients are, community organizing, many types of advocacy, and an emphasis on social change on multiple levels. Norman's life work exemplifies these values, perspectives, and actions.

Women Expelled from Sociology

In addition, he may also know that social work and sociology, which is his original academic field], were once part of the same discipline at the University of Chicago, USA, where social work and sociology began. In 1916, the men in the sociology department expelled the women in the department for their stances on social reform. They believed that research should inform the general public, and then the general public would bring about social reform. The women believed in both research and advocacy, and they did both, bringing about major federal legislation in the US, such as child labor laws.

Those expelled from the sociology department included Edith Abbott, Grace Abbott, and Sophinisba Breckinridge. Jane Addams was a frequent guest lecturer and a collaborator with many Chicago faculty. Professors from the University of Chicago, such as John Dewey, spent time at Hull House. See Bulmer (1984), Deegan (1990), Forte (2004), and Gilgun (1999, 2007, 2015), Hamington (2018). and Hart (2010)for more history.[KM8]

Karen and I did several pre-conference workshops together not only on EBP but also on navigating the academy as qualitative researchers. Roy Ruchdeschel joined us for some of the navigating workshops. By around the sixth year of the Congress, which was 2010, Norman wanted to develop communities of interest within the Congress, and so he invited the social workers he knew to organize Social Work Day (SWD), which would be a pre-conference session of papers, workshops, and roundtables.

Other pre-conference days that Norman encouraged included indigenous qualitative inquiry, a day in Portuguese and Spanish, a day in psychology, and a day in qualitative health research, among others. We were free to design the program as we wished, and we could have any many sessions as we had presenters.

Jumped at the Idea

At the social work gathering that year, we jumped at the idea and decided that I would become the organizer of SWD. We agreed that Karen eventually would take over the organization of SWD in a undesignated number of years as I was already a senior scholar and Karen was barely mid-career. When Karen became co-editor of Qualitative Social Work in 2012, we realized that she was no longer available to take over SWD. We agree that our involvement with the Congress led to our taking two different leadership paths: she as co-editor of Qualitative Social Work and I as the organizer/director/convener of SWD.

After the first SWD, Norman suggested to Karen and me that we put together a special issue of papers from SWD for one of the journals he edits. At each SWD, I bring up the opportunity to have a special collection. Until 2018, the energy had not been sufficient to go forward. This SWD, there was energy for a special collection. See the call for papers for a special issue of *Qualitative Social Work: Research and Practice.*

The First Social Work Day

The first Social Work Day was exciting for me, and I experienced excitement among the participants. I set up the program to build community as well as to share ideas, and, therefore, we had an opening and closing plenaries that were meant to bring out important ideas for qualitative inquiry in social work and to give people a chance to get to know one another. I made a video of the first SWD. Here is the link: https://www.youtube.com/edit?o=U&video_id=AiDGZ7tjr5M

Each year for the opening plenary, we have panels. I invite speakers who have critical perspectives, meaning they sought to understand power and privilege. While I often invite senior faculty, I also seek PhD students and new professors to be plenary speakers. I want to promote critical theories in social work, and I also want to promote the brilliant young scholars who do qualitative research. My goals for SWD are consistent with the goals that Norman has for ICQI.

Town Hall

At the end of each SWD, we have a Town Hall, where we discuss, sometimes in small groups, sometimes in large groups, our experiences of the day, what went well, what we can do better, and what we might plan for the following year. Over the years, participants raised recurring topics. This newsletter is a response to these discussions. We don't cover all of the topics in this issue, but I am confident we will in future issues--and from many points of view. These are the recurring topics.

Recurring Topics

- Mentoring new researchers and more seasoned people who want to do qualitative inquiry
- Desiring (and designing) more courses on qualitative inquiry in PhD programs
- Teaching qualitative research
- Developing [KM12]methods and methodologies that are social work-specific
- Funding qualitative research
- Critical theories and qualitative inquiry in social work
- Theory and qualitative research
- Creativity, innovation, humor, and playfulness in qualitative research social work
- Art-based inquiry
- Anger: Constructive responses to gatekeepers who don't understand and reject qualitative inquiry

- Funders
- IRBs
- Members of dissertation committees
- Senior faculty who vote on tenure
- Deans & directors
- Other faculty researchers
- Advocacy and qualitative inquiry
- History of qualitative research in social work
- Publishing articles based on qualitative approaches
- Innovative ways to disseminate findings

Looking Forward

Social Work Day is the great qualitative social work get-together. Social workers from throughout the world come together to share ideas and draw energy from each other. This is global gathering where scholars present cutting edge research using both traditional and innovative qualitative research methods and share new and emerging methodologies. We have a special interest in promoting the development of students, new scholars, and more seasoned scholars who have an interest in qualitative inquiry. We recognize that we benefit through the support and learning we experience at SWD.

Participants are from many countries, including Canada, Ghana, Mexico, Chile, the Caribbean, England, Norway, India, Australia, New Zealand, Hong Kong, China, Japan, Turkey, Brazil, USA, and others. We have a variety of interests, experiences, and perspectives, and we share a vision of a just and caring world. We engage in the challenging work needed to bring the vision to fruition, one local setting at a time.

I hope that SWD and this newsletter, *Qualitative Inquiry in Social Work*, continue to evolve and to be responsive to emerging issues related to social work and social welfare. We have taken on huge tasks as social workers, and joining together as we do at SWD is will increase our effectiveness.

Below I've listed on-line links to SWD programs from 2016 to 2018 and to videos on SWD and ICQI beginning in 2011.

Note: Many thanks to Karen Staller for her comments on an earlier version of this article.

Links to SWD Programs

These are links to some of the recent SWD programs. Any money we make from the programs goes into the SWD treasury for expenses such as tea and coffee for SWD. We currently have $300.

2016 Program
https://www.amazon.com/Social-Work-Day-Program-International-ebook/dp/B01FNPMJDW/ref=sr_1_3?s=digital-text&ie=UTF8&qid=1532183756&sr=1-3&keywords=Social+Work+Day+Gilgun

2017 Program
https://www.amazon.com/dp/B0713YW124/ref=dp-kindle-redirect?_encoding=UTF8&btkr=1

2018 Program
https://www.amazon.com/Social-Work-Day-2018-International-ebook/dp/B07CW4Y4DQ/ref=sr_1_2?s=digital-text&ie=UTF8&qid=1532183756&sr=1-2&keywords=Social+Work+Day+Gilgun

Videos from SWD and ICQI

I also made videos for several SWDs and for the Congress. The titles and links are below.

2011
Social Work Day
https://www.youtube.com/edit?o=U&video_id=AiDGZ7tjr5M

Opening Address: International Congress of Qualitative Inquiry by Norman Denzin
https://www.youtube.com/edit?o=U&video_id=H7y1zILQOPg
Social Work Researcher Michal Krumer-Nevo's Keynote Speech on Writing Against Othering
https://www.youtube.com/watch?v=KiJpyeWJAC8 Part 1
https://www.youtube.com/watch?v=qdKnW7klE5g Part 2

2012
Social Work Day
http://www.youtube.com/watch?v=kD_Ymc76ypU

The Usefulness of Intervention Research in Social Work by Melissa Solas
https://www.youtube.com/watch?v=f_gB50GSeHs

Into the Mouth of the Dragon: Secondary Trauma & Qualitative Research by Jane Gilgun
https://www.youtube.com/watch?v=EPSv97V0u4U

The Current Crisis in Social Services by Karen Staller
https://www.youtube.com/edit?o=U&video_id=l3oavRJRGkc

Tributes to Roy Ruchdeschel as he Bids Farewell as Co-Editor of Qualitative Social Work
https://www.youtube.com/watch?v=nHNLRUni3ys

2014
Social Work Day
https://www.youtube.com/watch?v=SNu5fx7r6t8

The Meanings of Violence to Perpetrators by Jane Gilgun
https://www.youtube.com/edit?o=U&video_id=xhq-YcCI5tY

Barbeque & Dance: International Congress of Qualitative Inquiry
https://www.youtube.com/watch?v=vXNP6LlEVzo

2016
Social Work Day
https://www.youtube.com/edit?o=U&video_id=FWqtSp6CAGo

2017
Deductive Qualitative Analysis & the Search for Black Swans by Jane Gilgun https://www.youtube.com/edit?o=U&video_id=MYubj5cYlD8

Citations
Deegan, Mary Jo. (1990). *Jane Addams and the men of the Chicago School, 1892-1918*. New Brunswick, N. J.: Transaction.

Forte, James A. (2004). Symbolic interactionism and social work: A forgotten legacy. Part 1. *Families in Society, 85(3)*, 391-400.

Gilgun, Jane F. (1999). Methodological pluralism and qualitative family research. In Suzanne K. Steinmetz, Marvin B. Sussman, and Gary W. Peterson (Eds.), *Handbook of Marriage and the Family* (2nd ed.) (pp. 219-261). New York: Plenum

Gilgun, Jane F. (2007, November). The legacy of the Chicago School of Sociology for family theory-building." Paper presented at the pre-conference workshop on theory construction and research methodology, National Council on Family Relation, Pittsburgh, PA, USA.

Gilgun, Jane F. (2015). *Chicago School traditions: Deductive Qualitative Analysis & grounded theory*. Amazon.

Hamington, Maurice (2018). Jane Addams. Stanford Encyclopedia of Philosophy. https://plato.stanford.edu/entries/addams-jane/

Hart, Chris (Ed.). (2010). *The legacy of the Chicago School. A collection of essays in honour of the Chicago School of Sociology during the first half of the 20th century*. Leeds: Midrash.

MEET THE EDITORS

Qualitative Inquiry in Social Work is a global newsletter with the purpose of sharing experiences that academic journals rarely publish, including stories of experiences and content sometimes transmitted orally in team meetings, teaching, and advising. The newsletter provides encouragement to researchers and other inquirers to write about their experiences. To fulfill the goal of being global, the editors of *Qualitative Inquiry in Social Work* represent many regions around the globe. They will represent the issues of the regions for which they are editors. We look to them for the identification of issues relevant to qualitative inquiry in social work and of persons to write about these issues. We are looking for editors in China, South Korea, North Korea, Japan, and other countries of the Pacific Rim. If you live in those regions, we want to receive expressions of interest to enhance our global reach. Meet the editors of *QISW*.

Jane F. Gilgun, professor, School of Social Work, University of Minnesota, Twin Cities, USA, editor, jgilgun@umn.edu. In consultation with

other editors, Jane will oversee the policies, the content, and the reach of the newsletter. She will write occasional pieces, news items, and essays as well as encourage others to write about their experiences. Jane began doing qualitative inquiry in social work as a PhD student in child and family studies at Syracuse University in the early 1980s. She remembers being surprised to learn that we can do research by interviewing people. She realized that she had been interviewing people for years as a social worker and as a student journalist. Coincidence or not, she found that almost all of the research questions that interested her were answerable through qualitative interviewing.

Anindita Bhattacharya, PhD Candidate, Columbia University, New York, USA, editor for South Asia. ab4050@columbia.edu Anindita's biog-

raphy and her qualitative inquiry are connected as the article she wrote for *QISW* shows. Anindita will represent the interests of South Asia by letting people know about *Qualitative Inquiry in Social Work*, forwarding copies of the newsletter to people who may be interested, soliciting articles for the newsletter, and anything else she might decide to do.

David Camacho, PhD student, Columbia University, New York, USA, editor for Mexico & Central America, http://dc3027@columbia.edu. Da-

vid will represent the interests of that region of the world by letting people know about *Qualitative Inquiry in Social Work*, forwarding copies of the newsletter to people who may be interested, soliciting articles for the newsletter, and anything else he might decide to do. David wrote a reflection for this issue of *QISW* where he reflected upon power, race, oppression and privilege and their effects.

César A. Cisneros Puebla, professor, Autonomous Metropolitan University, Iztapalapam Mexico, global roving editor.

cesar41_4@hotmail.com Cesar is a world traveler, and he will represent *Qualitative Inquiry in Social Work* globally. He will let people know about *Qualitative Inquiry in Social Work*, forward copies of the newsletter to people who may be interested, solicit articles for the newsletter, and anything else he might decide to do.

Jim Drisko, professor, Smith College, Northampton, USA, roving global editor, jdrisko@smith.edu Jim travels a great deal and will represent the

interests of *Qualitative Inquiry in Social Work* both in his travels and at home. He teaches practice and research courses and has written on topics of qualitative research methods, evidence-based practice, on reactive attachment disorder, and child psychotherapy practice. He was elected to the National Academies of Practice in Social Work in 2008 and was named an inaugural Fellow of the Society for Social Work and Research in 2014. Jim wrote an essay on qualitative inquiry.

Guy Enosh, associate professor, University of Haifa, Israel, editor for the Middle East. enosh@research.haifa.ac.il. Guy's research focuses on pro-

fessional decision making, causes and effects of interpersonal conflict and aggression, and research relationships/ethics. He serves as head of the Committee for Ethics in Research with Human Beings of the University of Haifa, and as academic director of University of Haifa programs for Ultra-Orthodox Jews. Guy will represent the interests of that region of the world. Guy wrote a reflection on Social Work Day.

Vanessa Jara-Labarthe, University of Tarapac, Chile, editor for South America. vanedk@gmail.com. Vanessa will represent the interests of that region of the world by letting people know about *Qualitative Inquiry in Social Work*, forwarding copies of the newsletter to people who may be interested, soliciting articles for the newsletter, and anything else she might decide to do.

Magnus Mfoafo-M'Carthy, associate professor, Wilfrid Laurier University, Kitchner, Ontario, Canada, roving editor for global mental health. mmfoafomcarthy@wlu.ca. Magnus will represent the interests of people with mental health issues globally. He travels widely and is thus well-positioned to advocate for the interests of people with mental health challenges. His research focuses on the perspectives of people with mental health issues, the stigma of mental health issues, service delivery, and policies both local and global.

Festus Moasun, PhD candidate, Wilfrid Laurier University, Kitchner, Ontario, Canada, editor for Ghana and West Africa moas3180@mylaurier.ca Festus has awareness of the social welfare issues in this region and will cover the African continent on specific issues such as poverty, disability, and child protection. Festus's main research interest is the meanings of the killing of children with disabilities in Ghana. He is not researching this topic for his dissertation because of concerns about the cultural awareness and sensitivity to Ghanian beliefs and practices of ethics review boards. See his article on ethics boards in this issue.

Debra Nelson-Gardell, associate professor, University of Alabama, Tuscaloosa, USA, editor for development. dnelsong@sw.ua.edu Debra is also coordinator of Ask Professor Debra, where she will receive questions that inquirers throughout the world have about their work. She will relay the questions to the other editors of the newsletter for their thoughts. She will often answer the questions herself as well. Debra will also focus on issues related to students and new professionals, such as preparation for proposal presentations and what to expect in job interviews. Deb's reflections on her identity as a social worker and on Social Work Day are in this issue.

Austin Oswald, PhD student, City University of New York, USA, roving editor for PhD students and new professionals. aoswald@gradcenter.cuny.edu Austin represents the interests of these young professional, serves as an ambassador for qualitative inquiry, and encourage them to write brief reflections. Austin reflected on his experiences at Social Work Day 2018 in an article for this edition of *QISW*.

Burcu Ozturk, PhD candidate, University of Alabama, Tuscaloosa, AL, USA, editor for Eastern Europe, bozturk@crimson.ua.edu Burcu will represent the interests of that region of the world by letting people know about *Qualitative Inquiry in Social Work*, forwarding copies of the newsletter to people who may be interested, soliciting articles for the newsletter, and anything else she might decide to do. Burcu wrote an article for the newsletter called Unheard Stories of Survivors of Intimate Partner Violence Among Immigrant Families in the United States

Tracie Rogers, assistant professor, University of the Southern Caribbean; editor for the Caribbean. tracie.rogers@gmail.com. Tracie will represent the interest of that region. Tracie is interested in power, privilege, and representation in social work research. Tracie is interested in the power, privilege, and representation. Tracie wrote a reflection for *QISW* about her experiences and perspectives as a Caribbean social worker called Engaging Self, Otherness, and Reflexivity in Social Work Academia:

Rita Sørly, Forsker, Norut Northern Research Institute, Tromsø, Norway, editor for the Nordic countries,mailto:rita.sorly@norut.no Rita will represent the interests of that region of the world by letting people know about *Qualitative Inquiry in Social Work*, forwarding copies of the newsletter to people who may be interested, soliciting articles for the newsletter, and anything else she might decide to do. Rita wrote two articles for the newsletter: one about health issues of the indigenous Sami people in Norway and the other on becoming a journal editor.

Sarah Vicary, senior lecturer, Open University, London, UK editor for Western Europe, mailto:sarah.vicary@open.ac.uk Sarah is happy to extend  the network of qualitative social work researchers across the Atlantic and beyond. She does research using interpretive phenomenological analysis. She is especially interested in drawing as a way to access research participants' thoughts, feelings and emotions that might otherwise be in accessible. Sarah wrote a reflection about these topics for this issue.

An Invitation to Write for *QISW*

Please consider writing for *Qualitative Inquiry in Social Work*. This first issue has more than 30 articles, suggesting that the newsletter has tapped into a grand desire to share our experiences as qualitative researchers and inquirers. As you can see from the articles, the writing is informal, first person, and compelling. Authors have shared some of their deepest experiences in ways that show courage, resistance, and desire for positive social change. We are accepting submissions for the second issue now. The deadline is 13 February 2019.

Reflexivity, which here means digging deeply into our experiences that we interpret through our understandings of social locations, is a theme of this issue and a calling that is part of being a social worker. Social workers have a vision of a just and caring world, and we take actions to bring about this vision. Our reflexivity frees us from—or helps us manage--self-doubts that hold us back. Our reflexivity empowers us to do something about unjust and uncaring everyday practices and policies. Our reflexivity helps us to identify with and connect to others with whom we have much in common even as we also have endearing differences that are mutually enriching.

Other themes of this first issue of *QISW* are the meanings and implications of race and gender, cultural sensitivity and awareness, meanings in context, relationships with research participants, the mutuality of research and inquiry, and the importance of global communities for social workers. You may identify other themes. Please write about your views for the next issue of *QISW*.

As said in the first article in this issue, *QISW* is a global publication whose goal is to promote global community among social workers. When we do this, we empower ourselves to continue to work for social and economic justice and care. As Freda Coleman-Reed said in her article, "social workers like myself, and others, have survived and thrived in the profession because we have gathered together and shared our experiences as social workers."

Articles that I'd like to see in *QISW* include descriptions of issues in our local settings and how qualitative inquiry has responded or could respond to them and accounts of stories that shaped us into becoming qualitative inquirers in social work. The next issue will have an emphasis on descriptions and reflections on local settings.

QISW is an outgrowth and extension of the community and generative of Social Work Day, the great, global qualitative social work get-together, that takes place each year as a pre-conference at the International Congress of Qualitative inquiry in Urbana, IL, USA. Social workers throughout the world gather each year at Social Work Day to share experiences and ideas and to draw energy from each other. A newsletter than continues the exchanges and community that we've are a logical outgrowth and extension of Social Work Day.

Articles can be brief, up to 500 words, or longer when authors want to offer an essay, as Jim Drisko, Rita Sørly, and I did. They can take the form of poetry, performances, videos, websites, and photographs.

Send your articles to me, Jane Gilgun, at jgilgun@umn.edu. If you have some ideas for articles and would like some feedback, please email me or Debra Nelson-Gardell, development editor, dnelsong@sw.ua.edu. We are happy to work with authors on their ideas for articles.

Remember, for the next issue, articles are due on 13 February 2019. We are accepting submissions now.

Jane Gilgun
jgilgun@umn.edu

Guidelines for Writing for *QISW*

"Grab" fits the kind of writing we do for *Qualitative Inquiry in Social Work*. Grab means the writing is interesting and memorable, and it hooks readers into the narratives. It also means that authors share what their topics mean to them and, if they are discussing their research, what the research means to participants.

In *QISW*, for articles, we'd like the first sentence to contain the topic of the article and that the sentence be written in such a way that it grabs readers' attention. Austin Oswald's opening sentence is his reflection is an example: "Attending Social Work Day was a profound moment...."

It's fairly easy to make writing about qualitative research interesting. We report what participants say and share our responses. When we get what informants are telling us, our writing is automatically interesting. When we dig deep into our own experiences our narratives become compelling.

First Person

We write in the first person. This is part of grab. Many authors believe that a more facts-based approach presented through a distanced, third-person voice is the way we're supposed to write. Donna Harraway called this the "god trick."

Grab is traditional in the Chicago School of Sociology, which flourished in the early part of the twentieth century, and to which social workers at Hull House made contributions. For example, professors at the Chicago School urged their students to read novels in preparation for writing up research.

Both memorable writing and the Chicago School are part of social work's legacy. The legacy is alive today. *Qualitative Inquiry in Social Work* is part of this living legacy.

Critical Thinking

Articles in *QISW* will also follow the principles of critical thinking, which is fairly easy for us because good qualitative inquiry employs these principles. The principles include general statements supported with evidence, examples, and elaborations, even-handedness in presenting multiple points of view, showing exceptions to general statements, showing connections between ideas discussed, and open-endedness that shows that we know that what we find is subject to further elaborations, and much more. We will add to this list.

Citations and Sources

Please use first and last name of authors and use complete citations. APA style or other recognized styles are fine. We will use the hanging first line.

In *QISW*, we put qualitative research in the forefront and will not engage in negative comments about quantitative research. Doing so distracts from the importance of qualitative research to social work.

Fine Points of Grammar

- The period goes inside quotes as in "horses."
- Use Oxford commas. This means a series of three has three commas as in "horses, birds, and fish" and not "horses, birds and fish."
- Use complete sentences as much as possible
- No run-on sentences. This is incorrect: It's foggy out, we will not have a picnic. This is correct: It's foggy out. We will not have a picnic.

Sources

Gilgun, Jane F. (2014). Writing up qualitative research. In Patricia Leavy (Ed.). *The Oxford handbook of qualitative research methods* (pp. 658-676). New York: Oxford University

Gilgun, Jane F. (2015). Research and theory building in social work. In William Nichols (Ed.), *Encyclopedia of Social and Behavioral Sciences* (2nd ed.) (pp. 502-507. New York: Elselvier.

Glaser, Barney (1978). *Theoretical sensitivity*. Mill Valley, CA: Sociology Press. Glaser is the first to use the term "grab," as far as I know.

Haraway, Donna. (1988). Situated knowledge. *Feminist Studies, 14*, 575-599.

Park, Robert E. & Ernest W. Burgess (Eds.). (1921). *Introduction to the science of sociology*. Chicago: University of Chicago Press. *These authors urged researchers to read novels as preparation for writing up research.*

Note: The guidelines are subject to revision

What's Going on n Your Home Regions?

The next issue of *Qualitative Inquiry in Social Work* will have a special section on What's Going on in Your Home Regions. This is an invitation to authors to describe and reflect upon local issues that are important to them and that are relevant to qualitative inquiry in social work. We are taking submissions now, and the deadline is 13 February 2019. They can be from 250 to 1000 words. If your piece is longer than 1000 words, please contact Jane Gilgun at jgilgun@umn.edu. Besides articles, submissions may also be in the form of poetry, performances, videos, websites, and photographs.

The issues can be social problems and instances of unjust and uncaring policies and programs, or the authors may choose to describe and reflect upon just and caring programs and policies. The articles are, first, to describe the situation and then show how qualitative inquiry can promote human well-being. If authors describe just and caring programs and policies or if the description is of something going well, then the reflection will be on how qualitative inquiry contributed to the success. The descriptions are as important as the reflections. Reflections can include interpretations, connections to other social issues, and even some informal references to existing research and theory, but these are not required.

In Minnesota, where I live, I am concerned about police killings of black men, the effects of racial discrimination on life chances of young people, and race-based disparities in school discipline, health care, housing, education, corrections, and child protection responses. Intersectionality of race and gender in law enforcement, the courts, and access to social services are also among my concerns. I see excellent, thoughtful collaborative social work going on in social service agencies and at the schools of social work in Minnesota.

These statements cover a lot of ground that I would elaborate upon. I would then reflect on how qualitative inquiry could respond and how I myself have responded in my research on the development of violent behaviors, the meanings of violence to perpetrators, and how persons overcome risks for violence.

I can't begin to imagine what qualitative inquirers globally will say about their local contexts, but I do know that as we talk to each other about what matters to us, our work and our lives will be enhanced. We will help each other work toward a just and caring world.

Other types of articles are always welcome, but for the next issue at least, we will specifically seek articles that describe and interpret our local contexts. We hope this will help us to begin to get to know one another and to build community. Another idea for articles is to tell stories that have shaped who you have become and what you do.

The articles on writing for *QISW* include guidelines and a description of the informal writing that we seek. Remember, we are accepting submissions now with the deadline of 13 February 2019.Email submissions to Jane Gilgun, editor, jgilgun@umn.edu.

Collages from Social Work Day & ICQI 2018

Social Work Day 2018

International Congress of Qualitative Inquiry, 18 May 2018

Social Work
Day

International Congress
of Qualitative Inquiry
17 May 2018

Social Work Day 2018

International
Congress of
Qualitative
Inquiry

ICQI 18, Karen Staller, Keynote Speaker

Kathy Charmaz, Sharlene Hesse Biber, Karen
Staller, & Jane Gilgun

Qualitative Inquiry in Social Work

ISBN-13: 978-1725028104

ISBN-10: 1725028107

First published in the United States in August 2018.